SECRETS OF THE PHARAOHS

Also by Ian McMahan

GET IT DONE! A GUIDE TO MOTIVATION, DETERMINATION, AND ACHIEVEMENT

FOOTWORK: A NOVEL

Avon Books are available at special quantity discounts for bulk purchases for sales promotions, premiums, fund raising or educational use. Special books, or book excerpts, can also be created to fit specific needs.

For details write or telephone the office of the Director of Special Markets, Avon Books, Inc., Dept. FP, 1350 Avenue of the Americas, New York, New York 10019, 1-800-238-0658.

SECRETS OF THE PHARAOHS

Ian McMahan

AVON BOOKS NEW YORK

AVON BOOKS, INC.
1350 Avenue of the Americas
New York, New York 10019

Front cover inset photo by National Geographic Society
Front cover background photo by Uniphoto
Interior design by Kellan Peck
Published by arrangement with the author
Visit our website at **http://www.AvonBooks.com**
ISBN: 0-380-79720-8

Library of Congress Cataloging in Publication Data:
McMahan, Ian.
Secrets of the Pharaohs / Ian McMahan.
p. cm.
1. Egypt—Civilization—To 332 B.C. 2. Egypt—Antiquities. I. Title.
DT61.M475 1998 98-26212
932—dc21 CIP

First Avon Books Trade Paperback Printing: November 1998

Printed in the U.S.A.

OPM 10 9 8 7 6 5 4 3 2 1

DEDICATED TO THE GENERATIONS OF EGYPTOLOGISTS
WHOSE WORK HAS BROUGHT
AN ANCIENT AND FASCINATING CIVILIZATION
BACK TO LIFE FOR US;
AND TO JANE AND SELENA
FOR THEIR ENCOURAGEMENT AND SUPPORT.

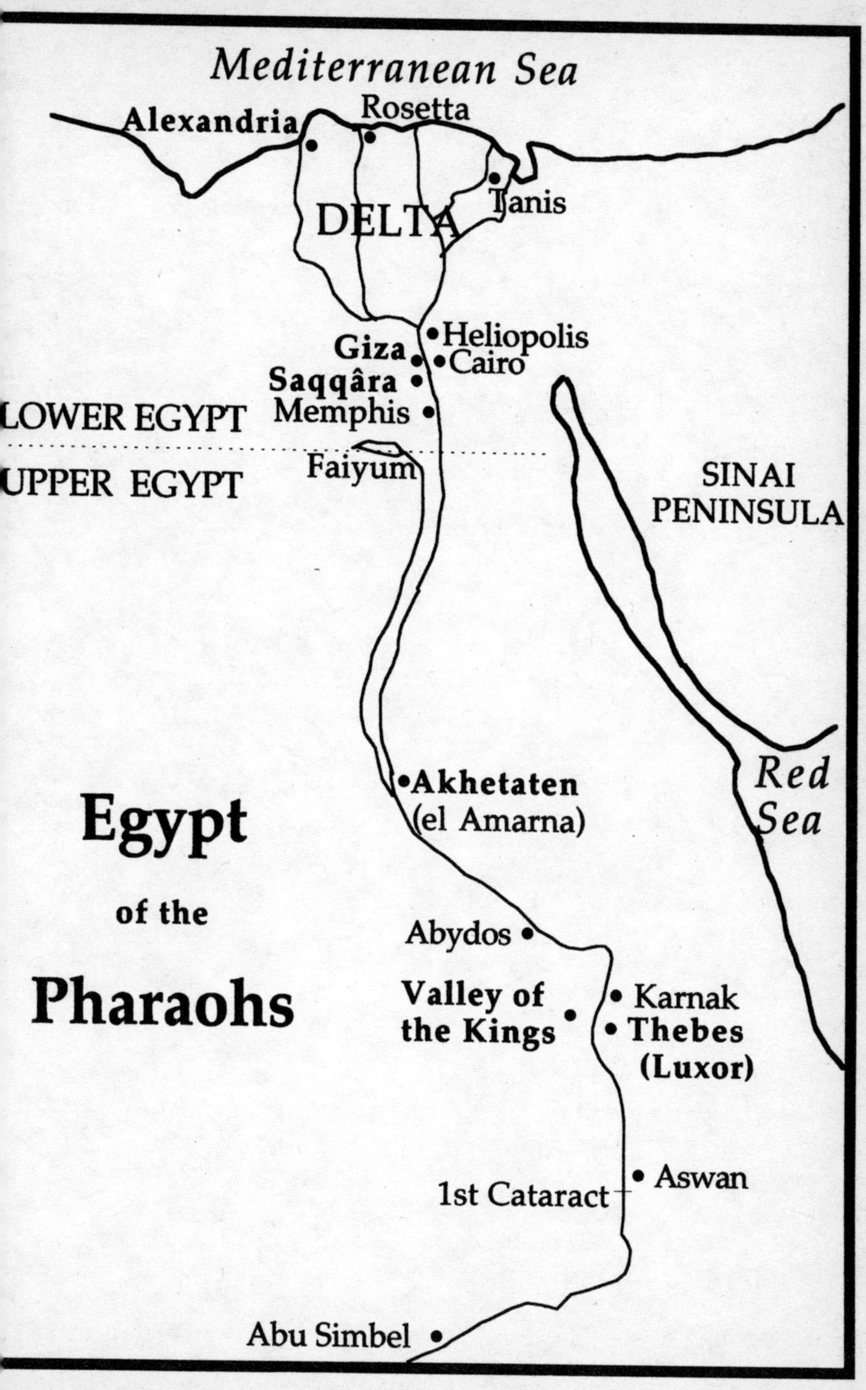
Mediterranean Sea
Alexandria
Rosetta
Tanis
DELTA
Heliopolis
Giza
Cairo
Saqqâra
LOWER EGYPT
Memphis
UPPER EGYPT
Faiyum
SINAI
PENINSULA
Red
Sea
Akhetaten
(el Amarna)
Egypt
of the
Pharaohs
Abydos
Valley of
the Kings
Karnak
Thebes
(Luxor)
Aswan
1st Cataract
Abu Simbel

CONTENTS

PART III
THE WONDERS OF THE WORLD

PART IV
THE REDISCOVERY OF EGYPT

SECRETS OF THE PHARAOHS

PART I

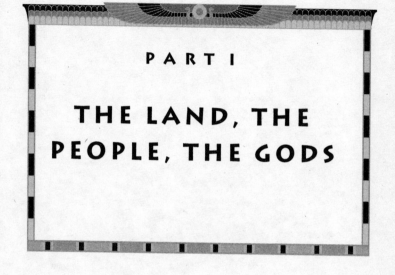

THE LAND, THE PEOPLE, THE GODS

TIME LINE

(All dates are approximate and are BC*)*

EGYPT		ELSEWHERE
Ivory and terra-cotta figurines placed in graves	3500	Rise of Sumerian culture in Babylon Development of cuneiform, earliest writing
	3400	
Glazed pottery and earthenware		
Earliest recorded dam at Memphis Hieroglyphs, paper made of papyrus	3300	
	3200	
Archaic Period (3150–2686) King Scorpion; Menes/Narmer; Upper & Lower Egypt united, with capital at Memphis; *1st, 2nd dynasties*	3100	
	3000	First wheeled vehicles in Sumer Megalithic monuments of Stonehenge and Avebury built in England
	2900	
	2800	Early Minoan culture on Crete
Probable starting date of calendar (2781)	2700	Beginnings of agriculture in China; legendary discovery of silk
Old Kingdom (2686–2181) *3rd dynasty*—Djoser's step pyramid at Saqqâra; Imhotep	2600	Epic of *Gilgamesh,* king of Uruk (2675)
4th dynasty—the Pyramid Age at Giza *5th dynasty*—cult of Re gains influence	2500	Cotton cultivated in Peru
	2400	

EGYPT		ELSEWHERE
6th dynasty—central authority weakened as regional rulers increase power; Pepi II on throne 94 years (2278–2184)	**2300**	Sargon I (2340–2280) founds Akkadian empire in Mesopotamia
	2200	
1st Intermediate Period (2181–2040) *7th–10th dynasties*—fragmented power rise of Thebes	**2100**	Earliest iron objects found in Mesopotamia
Middle Kingdom (2040–1782) *11th, 12th dynasties*—Mentuhotep restores power of throne; increased foreign trade; irrigation projects in the Faiyûm	**2000**	Palace of Knossos built on Crete Mycenaeans arrive in Greece
	1900	Abraham leaves Ur for Palestine Celts bring Bronze Age to central, western Europe
2nd Intermediate Period (1782–1570) *13th dynasty*—weak rulers, short reigns	**1800**	Hammurabi, lawgiver, king of Babylonia
14th dynasty—Delta separatists	**1700**	Shang dynasty in China (1760–1122) Earthquake destroys Knossos
Hyksos invade (1663) and rule as *15th dynasty;* Theban revolt led by Sequenenre (1574) and Kamose (1573–1570)	**1600**	Knossos rebuilt, height of Minoan culture
New Kingdom (1570–1070)	**1500**	Massive volcanic explosion on Thera (1470) destroys Minoan empire
18th dynasty—Ahmose the Liberator, Thutmose I–III, Hatshepsut, Amenhotep I–III, Akhenaten, Tutankhamen	**1400**	Iron Age begins in Armenia
19th dynasty—Ramses I, Seti I; Ramses II wins battle of Kadesh (1275), rules 67 years, has over 100 sons	**1300**	Shalmaneser I of Assyria founds Nimrud Possible date of Exodus led by Moses
20th dynasty—Ramses III; Invasion of "Sea People," economic and political troubles;	**1200**	Trojan War, destruction of Troy (1200) Nebuchadnezzar I, king of Babylonia (1146–1123)
high priest Herihor takes power at Thebes	**1100**	Fall of Mycenaean Empire to Dorian invaders

EGYPT		ELSEWHERE
	1100	Phoenician colonies in western Mediterranean
		David, king of Israel and Judah (1000–960), succeeded by Solomon (960–925)
3rd Intermediate Period (1069–525)	1000	*Iliad* and *Odyssey,* ascribed to Homer
21st–24th dynasties—turbulence and fragmentation; Meshwesh (Libyans) take the throne; Sheshonk I mentioned in Bible as capturing Jerusalem	900	Phoenicians import tin from mines in Cornwall
		1st Olympics, start of Greek calendar (776)
25th dynasty—Piankhi, king of Cush, becomes pharaoh; Assyrian invasions, Memphis and Thebes destroyed (667–663)	800	Legendary founding of Rome (753)
		Greek colonies in Sicily and southern Italy
26th dynasty—Saite period, attempt to revive earlier culture; growing influence of Greek mercenaries and traders	700	Solon, Athenian lawgiver (640–560)
	600	Medes conquer Nineveh, end Assyrian Empire
		Cyrus the Great founds Persian Empire
"Late" Period (525–332)	500	Rome declared a republic
27th–31st dynasties—Persian rule, revolt, 2nd Persian invasion; Alexander the Great defeats Persians, conquers Egypt (332)		Persia invades Greece (490–449), thrown back
	400	Wars between Athens and Sparta (431–404)
		Alexander (356–323) conquers Persian Empire
Greek Period (332–30)	300	Rome conquers Etruscans (295), rules Italy
Ptolemaic dynasty—Alexandria founded; Greeks become dominant over Egyptians; increasing influence of Rome. Antony, Cleopatra lose at Actium, commit suicide (30); Egypt becomes a Roman province		Great Wall built in China (220)
	200	2nd Punic War, defeat of Hannibal (209–201)
	100	3rd Punic War, Rome destroys Carthage and massacres its inhabitants (149–146)
		Julius Caesar takes power, is assassinated (44)
	1BC	Birth of Jesus of Nazareth (4 BC)

THE GIFT OF THE NILE

When Julius Caesar went to Egypt in 48 BC, he was the leader of a military expedition against one of his rivals for power. He was also a pilgrim, paying his respects to the world's oldest civilization. For the Romans, as for the Greeks before them, Egypt was the land where humans had first learned the names of the gods. Here people had invented the alphabet, learned to do complex calculations, domesticated wild animals, developed irrigation, and constructed the first buildings in stone. And what buildings—temples, tombs, colossal statues and obelisks so huge and elaborate that the gods themselves must have helped put them up!

Many of these great buildings were of an age that could scarcely be imagined. In the temples, scrolls and wall paintings listed the names and accomplishments of all the pharaohs, in a line that went back almost to the beginning of time. Julius Caesar may have already had an ambition to create an empire centered on his home city of Rome, but even he could hardly have dared hope to build anything as lasting as the Egypt of the pharaohs. After all, we at the end of the 20th century are a thousand years closer in time to Julius Caesar than he was to the earliest known rulers of Egypt.

To understand better the immense sweep of time that ancient Egypt covered, consider the following graph, which shows the life span of ancient Egypt compared to those of some other world powers across history.

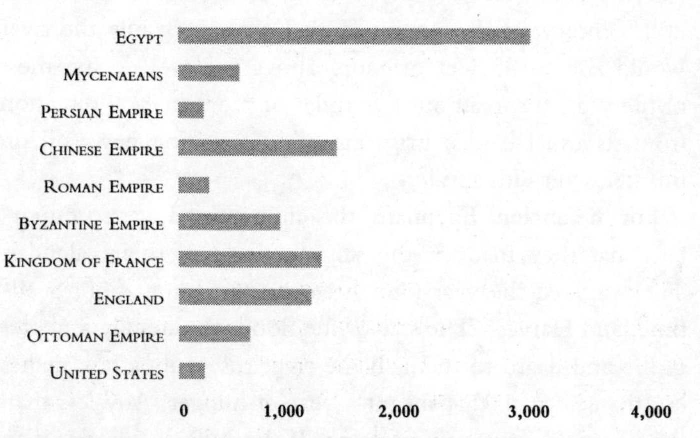

THE SURVIVAL (IN YEARS) OF SOME MAJOR WORLD POWERS

BLACK LAND AND RED LAND

On a map of the world, Egypt looks like a rectangle, roughly one and a half times the size of Texas. While strictly corrrect, such a map is also seriously misleading. In reality, Egypt—today, as in ancient times—is a narrow ribbon of life, laid across a vast, uninhabitable desert. That ribbon is the valley of the Nile River, hundreds of miles long but only a few miles wide. Although it makes up a tiny fraction of the country, the Nile Valley contains nearly all the fertile land and all the population. People have been saying it for 2,500 years or more, and it is still true: Egypt is the gift of the Nile.

The Nile Valley is an immensely long canyon, carved out over aeons by the river on its way northward to the sea. The sources of the Nile are thousands of miles south, in the tablelands of central Africa. From late spring into summer, heavy monsoon rains from the Indian Ocean drench these areas. The waters drain into the Nile and rush downstream, carrying along fertile topsoil. Until the construction, in the 20th century, of the Aswan High Dam, every July the river would rise to 25 feet or more above its level during most of the year. It spread out five miles or more in each direction from its usual banks, irrigating and depositing new soil on the fields on either side.

For the ancient Egyptians, this annual flood was so important that they made it the starting point of their calendar. They divided the year into three seasons: Inundation, Seedtime, and Harvest. The size of the flood was literally a matter of life and death to them. If the river rose only a few inches less than normal, that meant a year of hunger. Any less than that meant a devastating famine. If the Nile rose more than usual, that, too, spelled disaster, as the raging waters washed away dikes and mud-brick villages.

According to legend, the floods were controlled by the ram–headed god Khnum, who sent them forth from a cavern under the island of Elephantine, near the southern border of Egypt. On Elephantine, near the temple of Khnum, a steep flight of 90 precisely measured steps led from the heights to the low water level. This was the Nilometer, used to measure the rate at which the river was rising and to forecast what height it would reach.

The Greek historian Herodotus, who visited Egypt in about 450 BC, commented that the Egyptians did everything different from other people. If so, maybe it was because the basis of life in Egypt was so different from anywhere else. In other parts of the world, crops depended on the weather, which changed from day to day. Sometimes the sun shone, sometimes clouds covered the sky, sometimes it rained. Plowed fields lay next to meadows that in turn were bordered by wooded hillsides. If you wanted contact with other people, you might follow a path or rough track in any direction and come to a town, village, or hamlet. If you wanted to keep others from your land, you had to stay always on guard along your borders.

In Egypt, however, it almost never rained. Each day dawned as clear and sunny as the one before, and each night revealed an endless sea of stars. On earth, only two directions really mattered: north along the river, and south along the river. When you traveled, it was by boat, carried along by the current on northward journeys and by the prevailing northerly winds when you returned upstream. To east and west, the rich black soil deposited by the Nile went as far as the highest level reached by the annual flood. Just beyond, with no transition at all, was barren red sand. You could stand with one foot in a green field and the other in a desert that stretched for hundreds of miles.

The desert was more than a constant presence; it was also a guardian. Now and then, strangers might come in from the desert by ones and twos, but no invading army could hope to cross it and survive. To the south, beyond Elephantine, the river highway was blocked by a series of cataracts—rapids and falls impassable by boats. At its northern end, it emptied into what Egyptians called the "Big Green"—the Mediterranean Sea. For hundreds of years, until other peoples finally dared to sail across open waters, out of sight of land, this border, too, was safe.

Throughout its history, Egypt has been divided between

the Black Land—the fertile Nile Valley—and the Red Land—the surrounding desert. It is also divided in another sense. For most of its length, from the First Cataract at Elephantine to near present-day Cairo, the river is edged by narrow terraces that rise gradually to the base of sheer cliffs. Near the sea, however, the land becomes flatter and marshier, and the river spreads out into several branches.

Because its triangular shape reminded them of the fourth letter of their alphabet, the Greeks called this marshy area at the mouth of the Nile the Delta. The Egyptians knew it as Lower Egypt. The long, narrow valley to the south, they called Upper Egypt. These names make perfect sense when we remember that the Nile flows from south to north. Upper Egypt is upstream, and Lower Egypt is downstream.

Most of what we know today about ancient Egypt concerns Upper Egypt, and most of what we know about Upper Egypt concerns the Red Land, the barren stretches where the culture built its temples and its tombs. The reason for this is simple. The heat and dryness of the desert rocks and sand have preserved scrolls, fabrics, wall paintings, and even flesh from thousands of years ago. During those same thousands of years, however, the Nile has annually flooded, then buried under a new layer of soil, whatever souvenirs were left in the Black Land and the Delta.

People today often think of ancient Egypt as a culture preoccupied by death and the afterlife. This is a terrible distortion. It stems from the difference between the preserving qualities of the areas where the Egyptians buried their dead and the destructive effects of the river on the areas where they lived their lives. Imagine if, a thousand years from now, the most prominent remains of the United States were some cemeteries, war memorials, and monuments to dead presidents. That is something like our situation when we consider the Egypt of 3,000 years ago.

Settling the Valley

Fifteen thousand years ago, what are today the deserts of North Africa were lush grasslands and forests where herds of elephants, rhinoceroses, and wild cattle roamed. Most of Europe was still covered by glaciers. Then, for reasons that are still unclear, the global climate became warmer and drier. In Europe, the glaciers began to recede. In North Africa, long periods of drought began to transform the plains into desert. The animals, and the humans who lived by hunting them with stone–tipped weapons, started to withdraw toward the only dependable source of water left nearby, the river that flowed at the bottom of a long, deep canyon.

Humans had already lived in the river valley, in small numbers, for thousands of years. They had survived by hunting, fishing, and trapping birds in the reed–choked marshes that lined the river, and by gathering wild grains. Now, as their numbers grew, they began to give up their temporary shelters and build more permanent villages of mud-brick huts.

What happened at that point to change human history? Did someone trip and spill a handful of wild barley on the rich black dirt, then come back weeks later and find new sprouts? Did this new idea of deliberately growing crops come to the valley from someplace else, perhaps Mesopotamia? All we know for sure is that over the next few thousand years, people in the area that would come to be known as Egypt turned themselves from hunters and berry pickers into farmers. They domesticated wild animals—pigs, goats, donkeys, oxen. They perfected flint tools and began to work with copper. Most important, they developed new ways of living with the river.

Living with the Nile was not easy for them. For most of the year, its teeming waters and marshes helped feed them, but come summer, everything changed. During the months of flood, gravel levees thrown up by the current still marked the line of the normal riverbed. Otherwise the valley became like a vast shallow lake, miles across. At the outer edges of the flood was only barren desert.

As the waters gradually receded, they left behind a new layer of rich, moist topsoil. This would have been ideal farming land, with enough rain. But there was no rain. The only source of water was the steadily retreating river. Under the constant semitropical sun, the new soil dried up. Any plants that had started to sprout withered. As for the inhabitants, they had no choice. They followed the narrowing river back to its usual banks and once again cleared small fields within easy reach of the life-giving water.

As a flooded river subsides, however, it always leaves behind pools and ponds on low-lying patches of ground. The dry warmth of the Nile Valley would have made these bodies of water evaporate quickly, but not before they gave people a revolutionary idea. What if the floodwaters could somehow be saved, then used later during the long dry season?

The natural mounds or levees along the river's verge provided a solution. They were above the level of all but the highest floods. That meant they were a reasonably safe place to settle and build villages. They also held back the receding floodwaters. By building dikes across the gaps between levees, the villagers could create basins to serve as reservoirs. From these reservoirs, ditches and canals could transport the water to distant fields. For the first time it was possible to grow crops on land farther back from the river.

Constructing and maintaining a system of dikes, embankments, and irrigation canals was not a job one farmer could do. It took the labor of an entire village, or even of several neighboring villages, and it took careful organization. Fortunately, as more land was brought under cultivation, farmers became able to raise more food than they needed for themselves and their immediate families. This surplus fed a growing body of officials and irrigation engineers. They in turn organized projects to bring still more land under cultivation, to store up seed for the following year's sowing, and in good years to put aside some of the surplus against the possibility of a bad year.

For hundreds of centuries, humans had had one overwhelming concern: to get enough food to survive. Planning for tomorrow, or for next year, is not easy if you are hungry today. But now, as people began to win a small margin of freedom from that constant struggle, they also began to specialize in their work. Some people like to farm, or hunt, or build houses. But what if I am particularly good at making pots or chipping flints or building reed boats? Why should I spend my time plowing a field or making mud bricks? I can give you some pots or flint axes or a boat, and you can give me bricks or food in exchange. If everyone in my own village has enough pots, what about in the next village up- or downriver? And if shaping pots day after day starts to get boring, I can keep myself interested by drawing designs on the pots or by molding a spare lump of clay into the shape of a hippo or a crocodile.

Organizing drainage and irrigation projects, keeping track of stores of grain, managing trade among communities strung out along the Nile—these were jobs that required communication and record keeping. Communication and record keeping were just as important to the priests who were charged with honoring the gods who sent the life-giving flood each year. A new invention, writing, met these needs. With it came the new profession of scribe. Along with a more effective way to send ordinary messages, people gained the means to preserve knowledge and pass it to others hundreds of miles away or many years separated in time. We today can read a story told 5,000 years ago, because some scribe wrote it down.

Organization, specialization, communication—all these vital elements in the development of Egyptian civilization ultimately grew out of the simple but urgent need to get the floodwaters of the Nile to places where they would do less harm and more good.

THE LIVES OF THE PEOPLE

In 1920 American archaeologist H. E. Winlock set out to clear and map a tomb at Deir el Bahri, near the ancient capital of Thebes. The tomb belonged to Meketre, an 11th-dynasty court official from around 2000 BC. Any treasures in the tomb had vanished centuries before, along with Meketre's mummy. In modern times, the tomb itself had already been explored twice, in 1895 and 1902. Still, Winlock hoped that the rubble choking the passages might hide some wall inscriptions that earlier researchers had overlooked.

What particularly attracted Winlock was the location of Meketre's tomb:

> *At court his influence must have been considerable, for he chose the choicest spot in the necropolis of his day, directly overlooking the place where his sovereign's own mortuary temple was being built. The site is weirdly impressive. The great buttressed cliffs of tawny limestone practically enclose a deep*

circus a quarter of a mile in diameter. High above, around the rim of the circus where the cliffs start vertically upward, are the black mouths of the tombs of the courtiers.

As they cleared the passages and chambers of the tomb, the team found little of interest—no statues, no important inscriptions. Then, on Wednesday, March 17, near quitting time, one of the Egyptian workers noticed that chips of stone from his hoe were trickling away into a crevice between the wall and the floor. Alerted, Winlock rushed to the scene, armed with a powerful flashlight. As he later wrote:

There was nothing for us to see but a ragged hole, but when one by one we lay flat on the ground and shot a beam of light into that crack, one of the most startling sights it is ever a digger's luck to see flashed before us. I was gazing down into the midst of a myriad of brightly painted little men going this way and that . . . A tall, slender girl gazed across at me perfectly composed. Little men with sticks in their upraised hands drove spotted oxen; rowers tugged at their oars in a fleet of boats, while one ship seemed foundering right in front of me with its bow balanced precariously in the air. And all of this busy going and coming was in uncanny silence, as though the distance back over the forty centuries I looked across was too great for even an echo to reach my ears.

Winlock and his team had stumbled upon a hidden room, crammed with models representing every aspect of everyday life on the estate of an important court official. The 24 models, now divided between New York's Metropolitan Museum and the Cairo Museum, include a bakery, a slaughterhouse, a weaving shop, a brewery, a carpentry shop . . . Each is complete with tiny figures going about their everyday occupations.

A high government functionary like Meketre must have been constantly traveling upriver and downriver on official business. It is no surprise that the models include several boats. Some have a sail hoisted, for the journey upriver. In others, rowers and a helmsman guide the boat downstream, with the current. On one, Meketre himself relaxes in a chair, sniffing a lotus blossom and listening to a singer and harpist. Nearby, ready to come alongside at mealtime, is a cook boat, with millers, bakers, and a larder stocked with hanging joints of meat and jars of wine and beer.

In another tableau, herdsmen use long sticks to drive their black and white spotted longhorn cattle. From the shade of a pillared porch, the master and four scribes watch and keep count of the herd. There is even a model of Meketre's private garden, with a tree-edged reflecting pool made of copper. "The trees, made of wood, have each little leaf carved and pegged in place," Winlock noted. "The fruit is not growing from the twigs, but from the main stems and branches, so that there shall be no doubt but that the sycamore fig is intended."

For Meketre, these models were meant to ensure that his life in the next world would not lack any important feature of his life in this. For us, they provide a wonderful window onto a world that vanished 4,000 years ago. Along with many other finds—statuettes, wall paintings, papyrus scrolls—they give us a priceless glimpse of everyday life in what has been called humankind's first civilization.

EVERYDAY LIFE

It is not always easy to find out how people lived during the time of the pharaohs. Of course, it was a long time ago, but there are other problems as well. The Egyptians built their "houses of eternity," or tombs, of enduring stone and placed them out of the way in the desert. Their homes were made of more perishable materials, sun-dried brick and wood, and placed near the river. Centuries of floods have washed them away, then deposited layer after layer of sediment on whatever was left. In addition, when the organic binders in mud bricks decay, they produce *sebakh,* a substance rich in nitrogen. Egyptian peasants have been digging up sebakh and using it as fertilizer for dozens of centuries. Whatever walls survived the floods have usually been long since dug up and spread on the fields.

As if these difficulties were not enough, most of the major cities of ancient Egypt are buried under more recent villages and towns. Even if an archaeologist were to somehow move the people who live there now away from a site and then dig down through many feet of dirt, there is not much chance that the damp soil would have left anything that a museum would want to display.

Most of what we do know comes from two ancient town sites that have been studied in depth. Unfortunately, neither of these is an ordinary town, so what we have learned from them may not apply totally to other towns. One, near the modern village of Amarna, is the new capital built by the pharaoh Akhenaten around 1345 BC, then abandoned and leveled after his death some 20 years later. (His story is retold in Chapter 6.) The other is Deir el Medina, a walled village in a dry, desolate wadi on the west side of the Nile, across from Thebes. For over 400 years, during the 18th and 19th dynasties, it was home to the stonecutters, masons, painters, and other craftsmen who built and decorated the royal tombs in the nearby Valley of the Kings.

Based on what has been found in these towns, the ordinary Egyptian family lived in crowded conditions and in close quarters with neighbors. An average house had four rooms on one floor and faced directly onto a narrow lane. Like the palaces of the pharaoh and high officials, it was built of mud brick. This makes a perfect building material for a treeless country with a dry climate. The Egyptian word for mud brick is *djebat.* Over several thousand years, the word made its way across North Africa to Spain, then to the Americas. By the time it (and the building material it names) reached the American Southwest, it had become known as *adobe.*

The walls of a typical house were as much as 20 inches thick, which helped protect the interior from the terrible heat of summer as well as the chilly nights of winter. The few small windows were placed high up, to let out warm air while keeping out the bright sunlight. Floors were generally pressed clay or brick tiles and were probably covered with reed mats. The inside walls were usually plastered and whitewashed, sometimes with painted decorations as well.

Inside the front door, a shallow front room may have been a workroom or a place to welcome guests. Just behind it was the largest room in the house, where the family ate and slept. A ledge along the walls served as a couch and bed platform. Behind that was a small kitchen, with a clay oven and a hollowed stone for grinding flour. There was no chimney. Smoke from the cook fire was expected to find its own way out by the tiny windows. The thick layer of soot found on ceiling beams, and also in the lungs of mummies, shows that much of the time it didn't. A fourth small room next to the kitchen may have been a storeroom or an extra bedroom, and a staircase led up to the flat roof, which served as extra living space and a cool place to sleep on hot summer nights.

An important official like Meketre lived very differently from this, of course. His sprawling villa of 20 to 30 rooms would have had a garden filled with choice flowers and trees and a reflecting pool like the little model found in his tomb.

Inside the house, reception rooms had brightly frescoed walls. The floor may have been painted to look like a pool with fish, floating lilies, and colorful waterfowl. Tall pillars carved and painted to look like trees supported the ceiling. The family's private quarters included bedrooms, sitting rooms, and even bathrooms with stone floors pierced by holes for the water to drain off into. In the outbuildings, the staff of servants would be busy grinding grain, baking bread, brewing beer, weaving and sewing cloth, and taking care of the many other needs of the establishment.

At the top of the housing ladder was the royal palace, which was nearly a small city in itself. In addition to one or more royal residences, it often included temples, housing for servants and court officials, storehouses, and military barracks. The centerpoint of all this was the throne room, where the pharaoh received high officials and dignitaries. Here the frescoes on the walls displayed, not flowers and animals, but a triumphant pharaoh with row upon row of enemy captives or episodes from the stories of the gods (of whom the pharaoh was considered one).

One thing even the royal palace lacked was running water. Wells, too, were unusual. Who would go to the expense of digging a well when there was always a reliable source of water not far away? So, beginning at dawn and continuing throughout the day, lines of people—mostly servant women—made their way down to the river to fill great water jugs that they balanced on their heads for the return journey. What with cooking, bathing, washing dishes and clothes, cleaning house, and quenching the constant thirst a dry, hot climate creates, there never seemed to be enough.

What did the people of ancient Egypt wear? The short answer is, not much. Because of the heat and constant sunlight, they did not need layers of clothing for warmth. The air of the Nile Valley is nearly as dry as that of the neighboring Sahara Desert, so the evaporation of sweat is the most effective way the body has to regulate its temperature there. Such an environment favors light, airy clothing, and as little of it as possible.

Some modern observers have called the Egyptians history's first nudists. This is misleading. Nudism is, at least in part, a reaction against a cultural standard that forces people to hide certain parts of the body. In Egypt there was no such standard. Physical modesty was not considered important. Children under 12 or so, boys and girls alike, wore nothing at all, or at most an amulet necklace and a ribbon or string of beads around the waist. Servant girls in wealthy households also went bare or wore a brief apron. Men working in the fields usually tied a triangular piece of cloth around their waists that covered their rumps but not the genitals. Those in messier occupations—boatmen, reed gatherers, brickmakers—often went naked.

As for the clothes that people did wear, the amazing fact is that they changed little over many centuries. If a time traveler had kidnapped a builder working on Khufu's pyramid in 2550 BC and dropped him off in the Thebes of Ramses II, over 1,200 years later, his garb would have looked a little old-fashioned, but not enough so to cause comment. By way of comparison, imagine that someone from the time of Charlemagne was spotted on today's Champs Elysées or in the local mall.

Egyptian men, whether commoner or noble, went barechested and wore a kilt—a length of linen cloth wrapped around the waist. The ends crossed over in front and were tied or tucked under a sash or belt at the hips. An engraving from around 3000 BC shows Narmer, the first pharaoh, in a very short kilt. Ordinary people continued to wear short kilts, but among aristocrats kilts gradually became longer and longer. By the time of the Middle Kingdom (about

2040–1782 BC), the kilts of the upper classes were nearly ankle length and held in place by broad inlaid belts with long streamers. Then, in the New Kingdom, came a fashion revolution for men: accordion pleats in their kilts.

Women's clothing was also simple: a form-fitting tunic or shift that began just below the bust and stopped at the ankles. Broad straps more or less covered the breasts. The most fashionable versions of this dress were made of delicate, almost transparent linen gauze. As with the men, by the time of the New Kingdom a more elaborate style had come into fashion. Now the dress had vertical rows of tiny accordion pleats. A pleated stole covered the shoulders and was tied in front, over the bust. It shouldn't be thought that this change in fashion was inspired by modesty, though. The dresses were still cut from the most transparent linen obtainable. What is more, they hung open in front, from just below the breasts down to the floor. Judging from statues and wall paintings, the usual custom was to wear nothing under them.

Both men and women, from the pharaoh on down, usually went barefoot. For special occasions they might put on sandals made of papyrus, which wore out quickly, or of leather, which lasted longer but cost more. In style, these sandals looked a lot like the flip-flops people wear at the beach today, with a thong between the first and second toes that joins a strap across the instep. The fancier versions had embroidery or inset stones decorating the straps. Sandals of gold and silver have occasionally turned up in royal tombs, but it is hard to believe that anyone, even a pharaoh, would wear such uncomfortable contraptions while still alive.

From the earliest days of the pharaohs, Egyptian men had clean-shaven faces. Either they shaved themselves, with a stone blade or, later, a copper razor, or they paid a visit to the village barber. To let your beard grow to stubble length was one of the customary signs of mourning; otherwise, you shaved. Occasionally a noble would allow himself a neatly trimmed mustache or even a tiny chin tuft, but they were exceptions.

The other exception was the king himself, who on solemn occasions wore a long, stiff artificial beard held on by a string around his ears. This was to show his kinship to the god Osiris, who was always shown with such a beard. When queen Hatshepsut, whose story is told in Chapter 6, decided to take the throne in her own name, one of her first acts was to tie the ceremonial beard of a pharaoh to her chin.

Only the king wore an artificial beard, but most women, and many men among the nobles, wore wigs. Their own hair, they cut short or wore in a shoulder-length bob. Children had their own special hairstyle; most of the hair was cut very short or even shaved off, but a long lock was left to hang down at the right, or occasionally the left, side. Cutting off this sidelock was part of the ceremony marking the passage from childhood to adulthood.

The wigs that adults wore were generally made of human hair and carefully kept in special chests. They were often elaborately curled, waved, and braided. Recently the remains of a wigmaker's workshop from the end of the 12th dynasty (about 1782 BC) were uncovered at Deir el Bahri, near Thebes. The find included tresses of hair, a net wig foundation, various tools, and even a model head with a diagram of a wig. There was also a small quantity of a brown powder that may have been used as a hair dye. If the customer didn't care for either black or brown, the wigmaker would probably have suggested a wig reddened with henna.

Egyptian women also used henna to color their nails, palms, and soles. It was not the only cosmetic in use. From the earliest times, women (and often men as well) boldly outlined their eyes with eye shadows of different colors. Minerals such as galena (dark gray) or malachite (green) were ground into a powder on a decorated slate palette, mixed with oil to form a paste, and applied with a small rod of stone, metal, or bone. If there was any left over, it was stored in tiny jars made of alabaster, faience, or glass. There is some evidence for the use of rouge and lipstick, too, but this is mentioned and shown so rarely that it must have been much less common than painting the eyelids.

Egyptian clothing, what there was of it, was almost always white. For color, people relied on jewelry. Even the poor could afford a necklace or bracelet of brightly colored ceramic or faience beads. The rich were limited only by the skill and imagination of their jewelers. Egyptian craftsmen were unusually expert in the use of granulated gold, tiny grains of gold fused onto a background of solid gold. They also specialized in mosaic work, setting small bits of faience or gemstone in a design outlined by fine gold wire. The death mask of Tutankhamen is a celebrated example of this technique.

One of the most common pieces of jewelry for both men and women was the *wesekh,* a wide, flexible collar made of concentric rows of cylindrical beads. In addition to faience, the beads were often made of gold and semiprecious stones—lapis lazuli, turquoise, carnelian, and others. The Egyptians were not familiar with precious gemstones such as diamonds, rubies, and emeralds.

A great deal of Egyptian jewelry had functions beyond just being decorative. It had religious or magical significance as well. Almost everyone, even babies, wore at least one amulet on a cord around the neck. The most common were the ankh, the loop-headed cross that symbolized life, the *udjat* or Eye of Horus, and the scarab beetle, symbol of resurrection.

In a kingdom, the most important piece of apparel or jewelry is the crown. No example of a pharaonic crown has come down to us. Perhaps as the symbol of the living god, they were thought to have such power that they were ritually destroyed at the death of a pharaoh. However, we do know very well what they looked like, from scrolls and tomb paintings.

The pharaoh had a choice of several different traditional crowns. Two of them came down from the earliest times. The Red Crown, a tall cylinder that rose to a point in the back, was originally the emblem of the Bee King, who ruled Lower Egypt in predynastic times. The Reed King, who ruled Upper Egypt, wore the tall, cone-shaped White Crown. When the two kingdoms were united, in about 3050 BC, the two crowns were also united, to form the Double Crown. The Blue Crown was worn in battle and may have started out as a protective helmet. A different sort of protection, worn on the front of the crown, was the gold uraeus or sacred cobra, the symbol of the king's power. It was said to spit poison at any enemy who dared approach the king. For everyday use, the pharaoh wore a linen headdress, often striped, that tucked behind the ears and was held in place by a gold band with the uraeus at the front.

The queen had her traditional headgear, too, which we know only from paintings and statues. The best-known today, because of the famous portrait bust, is the tall blue crown worn by Nefertiti. Far more common, however, was the vulture crown, in which wings made of gold wire and multicolored stones covered the sides of the head. This was often topped with the tall plumes and moon disk that represented the goddess Hathor.

At Mealtime

"A thousand of bread, a thousand of beer, a thousand of all good pure things, for [the departed]." Versions of this prayer appear on tomb walls from every era of Egyptian history. Bread and beer were the staples of Egyptian life, but they were not the only "good pure things" that appeared at mealtime. Even the poorest family could afford to add a stew of lentils, chickpeas, and beans, flavored with onions and garlic. Garlic was also served as a vegetable and highly valued for its reputed ability to keep off disease. For dessert there might be fruit—dates, sycamore figs, raisins—or a special bread flavored with sesame or aniseed.

The most common sort of bread was made from a kind of wheat called emmer, which is very hard to husk. First the grain was crushed with stone pestles on flat limestone mortars, usually by men, then ground again in a hollowed-out stone quern, by women. Even then it was not very fine, with bits of husk and even whole, uncracked grains in it. It also picked up a lot of sand and grit from the grinding process, so much so that dental X rays of mummies show badly worn back teeth that must have been very painful. The dough was kneaded with the hands or feet, then allowed to rise. Baking was done by the women in ordinary families. On noble estates, there were servants who specialized in the task.

Recently, in Giza, American archaeologist Mark Lehner discovered an ancient bakery that was apparently built around 2470 BC to service the construction crews building the pyramid of pharaoh Menkaure. Lehner and his colleagues set out to reproduce the baking process. Based on bas-reliefs of the period, they re-created tall, two-part clay baking pots. While the dough was rising in the oiled lower halves, the top halves were heated over a wood fire. Then the cone-shaped bottoms were nestled in the hot coals, and the top halves placed over them. Two hours later, the team was enjoying slices of freshly baked ancient Egyptian sourdough bread, from a recipe 4,500 years old.

The Greeks believed that the Egyptians had invented beer.

Whether this is so or not, jugs that once held beer have been found in tombs from 50 centuries ago. In earliest times, beer may have been made by mashing stale bread in water, letting it ferment, then filtering it. If so, it was probably rather weak, with lots of floating husks in it. In any case, the Egyptians soon discovered much better brewing techniques.

Recently an English archaeologist, Delwin Samuel, used electron microscopes to analyze the residue left in beer jugs from tombs of different eras. She found that the Egyptians used a malting process, letting the grains sprout and toasting them before making them into mash, then adding yeast to encourage fermentation. When Samuel and a co-worker used the recipe suggested by their results to re-create Egyptian beer, they found that it was a cloudy golden color, with a rich malty taste that had a hint of Chardonnay!

It is not too likely that Egyptians had Chardonnay in ancient times, but they certainly had plenty of wine. Grapevines were a feature of every garden. A tomb painting from the 18th dynasty shows five barefoot men in short kilts pressing grapes in a large square vat. They are holding on to ropes suspended from the ceiling to keep from being overcome by the fumes. After being filtered, the juice was left in fermentation vats, then siphoned into tall clay amphorae for aging and storage.

The best wine grapes grew in the Delta and along the Mediterranean coast. Wine from there traveled throughout the Nile Valley. Amphorae have been found that are marked with the type of grape, the vintage year, and the name of the vineyard, along with the seal of the scribe as a guarantee. It is easy to imagine that, then as today, wealthy connoisseurs bought up the choicest vintages for their collections and served them to their most important guests.

In the tomb of an Old Kingdom noble, archaeologists found an entire meal ready to be served. Along with the usual jugs of beer and wine, it included barley porridge, roasted quail, pigeon stew, beef ribs, boiled fish, and stewed fruit for dessert. The diet of the well-off differed most sharply from that of the average Egyptian in the presence of meat. On festive occasions, a wedding or a child's naming day, an ordinary family might slaughter a sheep or goat and invite all their friends and relatives over to share it. Poultry such as geese and ducks and fish from the Nile might show up on the table even more often. Beef, however, was out of the question. It was expensive, and more important, in the Egyptian climate it did not keep very long. Only a large (and wealthy) household could finish the meat from a slaughtered cow before it spoiled.

We do not have any cookbooks from the time of the pharaohs. A scribe was much too important a person to be bothered with writing down anything as commonplace as a recipe. In tomb paintings, however, we see cooks roasting and frying meat and poultry and preparing what looks like stew. For frying, either vegetable oil or fat was used. According to Herodotus, "Various birds, quails, duck, and small fowl are pickled and eaten uncooked; any other available birds and fish, unless deemed sacred, are eaten roasted or boiled."

For sweetening their dishes, the rich used honey. This was much too expensive for ordinary people, who used dates or fruit juice instead. For seasoning, there was salt from the Siwa oasis and a variety of spices, including coriander, cumin, fenugreek, marjoram, and thyme, but not pepper, which was unknown in Egypt until Roman times.

The average family ate its meals squatting around a low round table. The food was set down in the middle, in a common bowl, and everyone reached in with fingers or chunks of bread to take from it. At fancy banquets, guests were seated at little tables bright with fresh flowers and served on individual plates, but they, too, used their fingers. A drawing that has survived from the reign of Akhenaten shows one of the little princesses digging into a whole roast duck, Henry VIII style. After meals, people rinsed their hands, which must have been quite messy by then. Sometimes they also rinsed them before eating.

LOVE AND MARRIAGE

The love of my sister is on yonder bank,
And the river lies between;
A crocodile lurks on the sandbank.
But I'll go into the water
And wade through the waves.
My heart is strong on the water
And the waves are like land to my legs.
It is love of her that protects me,
As if she had cast a water-spell for me.

This poem is part of a cycle of love songs that has come down to us from about 1400 BC. Hardly any of the poetry of ancient Egypt has survived, but what there is shows that love and romance were not that much different from today. As another poem in the same cycle puts it,

I kiss her, her lips open,
And I am happy even without a beer.

As a children's jump-rope rhyme from our own century points out, "First comes love, Then comes marriage." This was probably as true (or as untrue) for the Egyptians as for us. The practice was for a young man who was far enough along in his career to support a family to go to a girl's parents and ask for her hand. It is not clear if her consent was considered very important. She was probably several years younger than her suitor. Few of the marriage contracts we have mention age, but from other documents it seems likely that most girls from ordinary families married soon after puberty, around the age of 14. It was different, of course, for those of royal blood. For dynastic reasons, princes and princesses might be officially wedded even as young children, and often to their own brothers or sisters.

Brother-sister marriages happened fairly often in the royal family, as a means of preserving the dynasty. However, contrary to the impression many people have today, they were quite unusual among ordinary Egyptians. Czech Egyptologist Jaroslav Cerny studied 490 marriages in which he was able to track down the names of the partners' parents. He found only two cases that even *might* have been brother-sister marriages, and there were doubts about both.

As for the phrase "The love of my sister," in the poem quoted earlier, by the time of the New Kingdom, the word for sister had also come to mean "beloved" or "wife." This is not so peculiar. Today we might call a sweetheart "my baby," without leading others to think that we are referring to an actual child.

Apparently the wedding, when it took place, was neither a religious nor a civil ceremony. The new couple stood up before their family and friends and announced that they were married. Then everyone celebrated. Afterward, the bride moved into her husband's house. Sharing a house with in-laws, then as now, was considered a poor idea.

Women in Egyptian society were relatively well off, compared to those in other ancient societies and in a good many more recent ones. However, they were not equal to men. With a few very rare exceptions, women could not be priests, scribes, or government officials, though there are records of women doctors. Unlike, say, Victorian England, Egyptian society gave women control of their own property, even after marriage, and allowed them to enter into contracts and file lawsuits. Their chief role, however, was to manage the household and produce children, especially male children.

A CHILD IN THE HOUSE

The birth of a son was a great occasion. For the parents, it meant there was someone who would support them in later life and give them the sort of funeral that would assure their life in the next world. If, after trying, a couple did not manage to have a son, the wife would sometimes get a slave girl for her husband, then adopt any children she might have.

Son or daughter, Egyptian babies were breast-fed for a long time, three years or more. When mothers left the house, they carried their youngest in a cloth sling in front or on the left hip. It is possible that the long period of breast-feeding helped space out pregnancies. It is fairly certain that it helped babies to survive. A survey of a cemetery in Abusir showed more deaths among three- to four-year-old children than among younger children, who would have still been breast-fed.

Like children anywhere, Egyptian children played with toys and enjoyed games. Their toys included tops, rattles, and dolls made of baked mud or bits of wood. There were even tiny mummies in mud coffins. Carved cats and crocodiles with jaws moved by a piece of string have survived. Kids played ball, ran races, danced, wrestled, and went swimming in the Nile. One tomb mural shows two girls holding friends by the arms and spinning them around, pigtails flying; the inscription calls the game "pressing the grapes."

Starting at the age of five or so, children also took part in work around the house and in the fields. They helped sow the seed and reap the harvest. One mural shows them bringing food to the workers in the field. Another shows two girls pulling each other's hair as they fight over a just-harvested sheaf of wheat. Still another shows a boy helping fishermen hang their catch to dry in the sun.

The education of children was mostly left to their parents. Any boy who wanted to be more than a peasant or craftsman would also have to go to a school for scribes, where he would learn to read and write in both hieroglyphs and the less formal hieratic script. There is a lot we do not know about these schools. At what age did boys start their formal education? How long did it last? Were girls ever allowed to attend? Who ran the schools—the local priesthood? The state? Did parents have to pay tuition fees, and if so, how high were they? Did a bright boy from a peasant family have any chance to go to school and rise to a higher position in society?

We do know that papyrus was too precious to let beginning students blotch it up. Instead, they had to practice their writing on smooth bits of broken pottery called ostraca. One irony is that while papyrus scrolls fall apart over the centuries, pottery is practically indestructible. As a result, we are more likely to be able to read the beginning efforts of Egyptian schoolboys than the polished works of their masters.

All Manner of Disease

The Egyptians were greatly envied by their neighbors in Syria, Greece, and Mesopotamia. Their country was rich and well fed. Famines did occur from time to time, when the annual Nile flood was unusually low, but most years there was enough and more. Egyptians were also usually spared their neighbors' constant fear of invasion and war. Their country's power and wealth, along with the natural barriers of the mineral-rich deserts that bordered the Nile Valley, protected them.

At the same time that the river and the desert brought wealth and security, however, they also brought danger. The khamsin, a hot, dry wind from the west, brought clouds of sand and grit that settled in the lungs and damaged them. Mosquitoes that infested the marshes transmitted malaria, and swarms of flies passed on dysentery, typhoid, and trachoma, an eye infection that could cause blindness.

Villagers constantly waded barefoot in the shallow canals and muddy fields. They had no way of knowing that tiny water snails harbored the larvae of the parasitic bilharzia worm, which could pass through even healthy human skin and cause severe anemia. Other parasites, such as tapeworms, threadworms, and liver flukes, were also common and have turned up in mummies. The overcrowding, lack of ventilation, and poor sanitation in the villages favored the spread of such infectious diseases as smallpox, tuberculosis, and polio. From time to time, fleas carried by rats caused outbreaks of deadly bubonic plague. In the fields and among the rocks lurked poisonous snakes and scorpions.

To combat all these perils, there was the medical profession. Egyptian doctors were famed throughout the ancient world. In the *Odyssey*, Homer says:

> *. . . Egypt, land where the teeming soil*
> *bears the richest yield of herbs in all the world;*
> *many health itself when mixed in the wine,*
> *and many deadly poison.*
> *Every man is a healer there, more skilled*
> *than any other men on earth—Egyptians born*
> *of the healing god himself.*

The legendary founder of Egyptian medicine, later deified as the god of healing, was Imhotep, who also designed the first great pyramid, the step pyramid of pharaoh Djoser (around 2650 BC). One of the Egyptian medical texts that has survived is a New Kingdom scroll that includes a copy of a much older work on diagnosing and treating injuries. The careful observation and description of symptoms, treatment, and prognosis make it a strong candidate for the title of the world's oldest scientific treatise. It is tempting to think that the lost original was written by Imhotep himself.

This surgical text is unusual. Most of the medical documents that have survived are miscellaneous collections of herbal remedies, prayers, and spells. Some of the ingredients mentioned—henbane, mandrake root—are known to have medicinal effects. Others, such as fresh dew or a burnt ass's hoof, seem unlikely to have done the patient any good. Children who were very sick were sometimes made to swallow a whole, skinned mouse. We know that the remedy did not always work, because the remains of such mice have turned up inside the mummies of children. With still other medications, we know the names of certain important ingredients, but we do not know what the names refer to.

However skilled Egyptian doctors were, most of their patients died very young. Studies of tombstones and temple records suggest that the average life expectancy for men was around 27 years. For women, who faced the additional dangers of childbirth, it was 22 years. The better living conditions and health care enjoyed by the upper class generally meant a longer life, but not by terribly much. The ideal life span—the equivalent of the biblical "threescore and ten"—was 110 years. One 6th-dynasty pharaoh, Pepi II, was said to have reached it. Maybe he really did; his reign lasted 94 years. Among the many mummies of pharaohs in the Cairo Museum, however, only one, Ramses II, lived past 55. Most died between the ages of 20 and 40.

THE LIVES OF THE GODS

Throughout history, people have wondered where they came from and what powers created and governed their world. For the Egyptians, the most widely accepted answer to these questions was embodied in the story of the Ennead, the ruling body of gods and goddesses.

In the Beginning, the waters of chaos covered the world. Then a mound of earth slowly made its appearance above the waters. This was the mound of Atum, the Creator. Atum was alone. From his own substance, by his own solitary act, he then gave life to Shu, the god of the air, and Tefnut, the goddess of the waters. From the mating of Shu and Tefnut came two children, Geb, the god of the earth, and Nut, the goddess of the sky. In turn, Geb and Nut had four children: Isis, Osiris, Set, and Nephthys. These nine made up the Ennead.

Now, when Osiris had grown to manhood, strong and handsome, he became king of Egypt and took his beautiful sister Isis as his wife. He brought the people out of savagery and taught them the arts of civilization. Set, his brother, who married Nephthys, came to bitterly envy the glory of Osiris. He searched for a way to displace him.

Osiris went off on a campaign. When he returned the victor, Set invited him and his followers to a great feast. At the evening's end, Set showed his guests a magnificent coffin and announced that he would award this prize to the one it best fitted. At his orders, the coffin had been secretly built to the exact dimensions of Osiris. The moment Osiris lay down inside it, Set and his followers sealed the lid and threw the coffin into the Nile. Then Set seized the throne as his own.

The coffin bearing Osiris floated to Byblos, in Phoenicia, where it became lodged inside a great tree that was made into a pillar of the palace of the local king. But Isis had not forgotten her husband and brother. Grieving, she searched the world for his corpse. When at last she found the coffin at Byblos, she brought it back to Egypt and hid it in the marshes. Opening it, she flung herself on the body of Osiris, beseeching her fellow gods to restore it to life.

Anubis, the protector of the dead, came to embalm Osiris. Before he did, Isis used her magic to revive the corpse long enough to become pregnant. Then Set, out hunting in the marshes, discovered the coffin with the body of Osiris. Furious, he ripped the body into fourteen pieces and scattered them throughout the land of Egypt.

After a long search, Isis found all but one of the pieces of her husband's body. The genitals had been devoured by a fish. Some versions of the story say that Isis buried each fragment of Osiris where she found it. The head was buried at Abydos, which became the city most sacred to Osiris. In other versions, Anubis reunited the pieces and wrapped them in linen bandages to become the first mummy. The *akh* or spirit of Osiris was resurrected by the gods and became the Lord of the West, the land of the dead.

In due course, Isis gave birth to a son, Horus, and made him swear to avenge the murder of his father. Once grown to manhood, he battled his uncle Set for many years, until at last the gods declared that he was the rightful and eternal king of Egypt. Thereafter, every pharaoh in turn was regarded as the living embodiment of Horus. When a pharaoh died, his *akh* was assimilated to Osiris, while his heir, the "Horus in the Nest," became Horus. Thus, unlike lesser lands that had earthly kings, Egypt was always ruled by a god.

The story of Isis and Osiris is one of the centerpoints of Egyptian religious beliefs. However, unlike most of the religions we are familiar with in today's world, Egyptian religion had many centerpoints. Atum was the creator, but so was the sun god, Re. Ptah, the god of crafts, first used a divine word to breathe life into man, but man was also formed from clay by the potter god, Khnum.

Even the most basic Egyptian beliefs refuse to be pinned down. Re was the sun god, but long before Horus was known as the son of Isis and Osiris, he was Harakhte, Horus of the Horizon, a sky god whose left eye was the sun and whose right eye was the moon. In his falcon shape, Horus carried the sun across the sky in his claws. But at the same time, Re carried the sun across the sky in his solar boat. Or was it Kephri, another creator god with the head of a beetle, who pushed the sun across the sky just as dung beetles push little balls of clay across the ground in front of them?

Some modern authorities have called the ancient Egyptians the most polytheistic people in history. Others have insisted that behind this appearance of polytheism was a deep current of monotheism, a belief in only one supreme being who takes many different forms and names. Whichever view is right, certainly Egyptians were acquainted with many gods.

Any educated person would be familiar with the names, attributes, stories, sacred animals, and sacred cities of as many as 80 gods.

Among so many others, there was jackal-headed Anubis, the god of embalming, and the dwarf god Bes, who helped couples get along, and Thoth, the protector of scribes, and Neith, the goddess of hunting and war, and Hathor, goddess of love, often shown as a smiling cow. Those who chose to worship a particular god, or more than one, were at liberty to do so, as long as they did not interfere with the worship of others. If they were from some other country and could not manage to find any Egyptian god that suited them, they were free to worship one from their old country. They might even end up making some Egyptian converts.

One Religion from Many

How did such a complex and yet tolerant system of polytheism arise? The details, and most of the evidence, are lost forever in the many centuries before the invention of writing. One likely account is that in predynastic times, the towns and villages up and down the Nile shared a few central religious stories but also had their own mythical founders and supernatural guardians. As larger and larger areas were unified, leading to more communication among different communities, these local dieties became assimilated to each other.

Suppose that an official from a large town was on a visit to a village he didn't know. In getting acquainted with the place, he would have been careful to ask which gods were held in especially high regard there. If the god named was not known to him, he would then ask what the god's attributes were. Being told this god conducts the dead to the underworld, he would say, "Ah, that must be your name for the god I know as Anubis." Then he would pass on any stories *he* knew about the jackal-headed god. If the local god's attributes did not sound familiar to him, he might tell the story of this god at his next stop and on his return home. Gradually the village's local god would become familiar to people in other areas as well, and there would be one more figure added to the Egyptian pantheon.

The earliest solid information we have about Egyptian religion dates to the early dynastic period, around 3000 BC. Many of the gods who were prominent later were already well established by then. In particular, the king was already identified with Horus; his most important title was the one referred to as his Horus-name. Curiously, his royal titles often incorporated the name of Horus's enemy, Set, as well.

Some scholars have taken the story of the battles between Horus and Set to mean that these gods are symbols for their origins: Horus and his father, Osiris, as gods native to the North, and Set as the warrior god of the South. From the story of the victory of Horus over Set, they conclude that at some point in predynastic times, northern followers of Horus conquered the southern followers of Set and imposed their version of the myth on them. The problem with this argument is that the only conquest we know about went the other way. The South conquered the North. Could there have been a much earlier conquest in the other direction? It is possible, but all we have for evidence is that same set of myths whose origin we are using the supposed conquest to explain. A more likely explanation is that the story of Horus and Set came first. Later, after the unification of Upper and Lower Egypt, the pharaoh was identified with Horus, the victor.

We know more about religion in the Old Kingdom because we have the Pyramid Texts, spells and invocations that were inscribed on the walls of burial chambers. Naturally these tell us more about those aspects of religion that relate to death and the afterlife than about those that concern everyday life. Still, the inscriptions do show that both the sun god Re and Osiris, who was identified with the constellation Orion, were important as gods of the dead. They were also both considered the divine fathers of the pharaoh, who was both the living Horus and the son of the sun.

The Pyramid Texts make it clear that the pharaoh was expected, on his death, to become one of the stars. "You shall bathe in the starry firmament . . . The imperishable stars have raised you aloft . . . You shall reach the sky as Orion, your *akh* shall be as effective as Sothis; be powerful, having power; be strong, having strength; may your *akh* stand among the gods as Horus who dwells in Iru." Sothis was the Egyptian name for Sirius, the Dog Star. The brightest star in the heavens, every year it disappeared below the horizon for 70 days, then reappeared in late June as the herald of the annual Nile flood.

It may seem strange to us that the Egyptians thought of their king as divine and destined to become a star. Didn't they realize that he had been born and would die in the ordinary, human way? As often happens with questions of belief, the answer seems to be: yes and no. Of course they knew that the person who wore the crown was a mortal. At the same time, however, they believed that at the instant of death, the old pharaoh became transfigured as Osiris, and his heir became the new living Horus. This had many benefits. As a god, Pharaoh was able to deal with his fellow gods as an equal. If the annual flood was lower than usual, he could speak directly to Hapi, the plump, hermaphroditic god who personified the Nile, and tell him that he had better do better next time. He could intercede with the other gods on behalf of his people. As for demons and such, as a god, he could *command* them.

During the Old Kingdom, the only person who was reasonably sure of immortality was the king. Even he had to brave many dangers and remember a bewildering assortment of spells and rites to win his place among the stars. As for his family members and close associates, they built their own tombs as near his as they could, in the hope that he might need them in the Other World and bring them along. We can only guess at what ordinary people believed about the afterlife. We do know that they buried their dead with beads, tools, and pots of food and drink, so they must have thought they had at least a chance at surviving death.

By the time of the Middle Kingdom, the cult of Osiris had spread throughout Egypt, offering the hope of immortality to everyone, king and commoner alike. Just as Osiris himself returned to life after his murder by his brother, Set, so he could bring others back to life, to live forever in his kingdom of the dead. The key to that kingdom was not wealth or importance, but a pure, unstained heart.

The Middle Kingdom saw another important religious development as well. Several dynasties of pharaohs came from a town in Upper Egypt called Thebes, where the most important local god was a mysterious figure named Amen. Amen's name means something like "The Hidden," and he may have started as a god of the wind, which has great power but is never seen. His wife, Mut, was a mother goddess, and his son, Khonsu, was the god of the moon.

As Thebes became a great city under the rule of the new Theban pharaohs, so Amen's importance grew and grew. His temple at Karnak, just north of Thebes, expanded and became rich. He was given the attributes of Re, the sun god, and came to be called Amen-Re. Later he also took on the qualities of another sun god, Horus of the Horizon, and became known as Amen-Re-Harakhte. By the time of the 18th dynasty, what had once been a local Theban god was worshiped throughout Egypt. He was now called the king of the gods and even, in some inscriptions, the only god and creator. In time his priests gained a power and importance that rivaled those of the pharaohs themselves.

By the time of the 18th dynasty, the political and religious dominance of the priests of Amen was firmly established. Then, in the 13th century BC, this dominance faced a mortal challenge from the pharaoh Akhenaten, who proclaimed a single, all-powerful god, the Aten. Akhenaten's monotheistic religious reforms revolutionized Egyptian culture but disintegrated after his death. His story is told in Chapter 6.

The religion of Egypt had a powerful influence in other countries as well. Egypt was seen as the oldest of cultures, so it followed that its gods were the oldest of gods. When Herodotus visited Egypt, around 450 BC, one of his favorite activities was trying to figure out which gods of his native Greece corresponded to each of the Egyptian gods. Among others, he decided that Amen was identical with Zeus, the most powerful god in the Greek pantheon.

Later in classical times, the celebrated seer in the temple of Amen-Re at the oasis of Siwa, in the desert west of the Nile Valley, came to be known among the Greeks as the oracle of Zeus Ammon. After the victory of his armies in 332 BC, Alexander the Great made a pilgrimage there to be crowned King of Egypt. When the Romans came along, they for their part called the temple the oracle of Jupiter Ammon. During this same period, certain Egyptian beliefs, especially the cult of Isis, spread throughout the Mediterranean world and beyond, as far as Mesopotamia to the east and the British provinces of the Roman Empire to the northwest.

IN THE TEMPLE

The center of religious life was the temple. Today visitors to Egypt often come away with the impression that ancient Egypt was nothing *but* temples. They are everywhere, and they are enormous, with thick stone walls, imposing gateways, and forests of pillars like gigantic trees. In many places there are whole cities of temples, one next to the other. Like the cities of the dead at Giza, Thebes, and Saqqâra, these temple complexes foster an image of the Egyptians as a gloomy, introspective people preoccupied with the gods, death, and the world to come. As we shall see, this was not at all the case.

One reason the temples were so large is that they combined many functions that made them central to the intellectual and economic life of the country. The sanctuary of the god was, of course, the most important element. However, a typical temple would also contain administrative headquarters for the many workshops and estates that belonged to the god, training schools for scribes, doctors, and government officials, a library, and something that resembled a public health clinic. The Houses of Life, attached to the most important temples, had functions like those of a major university and research institute. Scholars from all over the ancient world were drawn to these storehouses of ancient learning, including such giants of Greek thought as Plato and Democritus. Pythagoras, still celebrated for the Pythagorean theorem, spent over 20 years studying Egyptian approaches to geometry and mathematics.

Most of the temples that have survived were built during the New Kingdom or even later, during the Ptolemaic and Roman eras, but they were built according to a plan that was already centuries old. The approach to a temple, along a stone-paved avenue lined with sphinxes, was calculated to give the visitor a proper feeling of awe at the greatness of the god and his house. The gateway, or pylon, consisted of two towers with sloping sides and flat roofs. These were heavily carved and featured rows of gigantic statues.

The gate, between the towers, was usually flanked by obelisks, tall, slim columns rising to a pyramid-shaped top. Obelisks were made from a single block of granite and thickly carved with pictures and hieroglyphic inscriptions praising the pharaoh who had sponsored them. They could be as much as 100 feet (30 meters) tall and weigh as much as 320 tons. Many of them eventually ended up far from Egypt, in New York, London, Paris, Istanbul, and especially Rome. The largest of all, however, is still in the quarry at Aswan, where it was left unfinished after the workers discovered a flaw in the stone. If completed, it would have weighed a staggering 1,150 tons and been the largest single stone object ever made on earth.

Inside the gate was a courtyard open to the sky and flanked by colonnades. This led to a large roofed hall called the hypostyle, thick with columns and lit by rows of clerestory windows. The best-known and most imposing hypostyle is in the temple of Amen-Re at Karnak, which is described in Chapter 9. The hypostyle was the place where those who had business with the temple or with the god gathered. At the far end, closed off from the public by high doors of cedar and bronze, was the sanctuary itself, a rectangular, windowless room dominated by the shrine that housed the statue of the god. Only the priests and the most influential worshipers were allowed inside this sanctuary.

Today the ruined temples are sternly majestic, but remote and foreboding in the purity of their pale carved stone walls and columns. They were very different in ancient times. The walls, with their gigantic statues and relief figures of gods and kings, were painted in bright, almost blinding colors.

The obelisks were often covered in gold leaf or even in electrum, a glittering alloy of gold and silver that to the Egyptians was more precious than pure gold. From tall flagpoles mounted on the tops of the pylon towers, long, bright pennants waved in the breeze. Even the floors might be paved with silver and lapis lazuli.

Egyptian priests were not ministers who tended their flock or preachers who communicated revealed truth to believers and steered them into the paths of righteousness. Nor were they mainly concerned with mediating between the people and the god. Instead, their role was to make sure the temple was a comfortable, attractive place *for its god*. Through worship, services, and offerings, they tried to draw the god's spiritual presence and attention. It is significant that the Egyptian word for priest meant "slave of the god."

In order to be worthy to serve the god, the priest had to be purified. Priests were required to shave the entire body several times a week, including head hair, eyebrows, and even eyelashes. They wore clothes of especially fine linen, made in a fashion that dated back to the Old Kingdom, and white sandals. There were specific foods that they were not allowed to eat, such as pork, certain fish, garlic, and beans. The list was different depending on the god they served. Priests of Osiris, for example, could not eat any sort of fish, because of the belief that a fish had swallowed the severed genitals of Osiris. Priests could marry and have families, but they were expected to abstain from sex during the days just before their service in the temple.

Each morning before dawn, the priest had to bathe or sprinkle himself with water from a ritual pool, then rub oil onto his skin. Inside, he joined a procession carrying offerings of bread, wine, meat, fruit, and flowers, boxes of fine new robes, toiletries, and incense. The doors to the sanctuary had been sealed the night before with a clay seal. The priest in charge broke the seal and the company entered the sanctuary.

At the exact moment that the sun's disk appeared on the horizon, the priests and the "Singers of the God," a guild that had existed since predynastic times, intoned the dawn hymn, "Awake in peace, great god . . ." The head priest opened the stone shrine to reveal the statue of the god. Often this was cast in solid gold. As a haze of burning incense filled the room, the priests laid the god's breakfast on the altar. Naturally, the god consumed only the spiritual essence of the cakes, meat, fruit, and wine he was offered. The material part that was left over was later taken away for the use of the priests and temple staff. After breakfast, the god's statue was washed, rubbed with oil, clothed in a new kilt and tunic of the finest linen, and decked with jewels. Then the sanctuary was closed until sundown, when it was ritually cleaned, swept, and resealed for the night.

Ordinary people had little or nothing to do with these daily ceremonies. In times of illness or distress, they might go to a temple to offer a special gift to the god, perhaps accompanied by a little stone tablet explaining their need. Many of these inscribed tablets have been found in the ruins of temples. They might also go to pose a question to the god, such as "Will my wife conceive a son?" or "Is the calf I plan to buy healthy?" As a rule, the god said little more than yes or no.

Otherwise, the main contact commoners had with the god came during holidays. At these times the statue of the god was taken out of the sanctuary and carried in procession for everyone to see and honor. Some of these processions wound through the town and then returned to the temple. Others were more lengthy. Every year the statue of the goddess Hathor left her temple at Dendera to travel a hundred miles upstream for a two-week visit to the temple of her divine husband, Horus, at Edfu.

One of the most elaborate of these holidays was the *Opet* festival at Thebes, which took place during the annual flooding of the Nile. Watched by huge crowds and led by Pharaoh himself, 24 priests carried the statue of Amen from his temple at Karnak down to the temple's water stairs. There it was placed on a gilded barge and towed upriver to the god's temple at Luxor. Nobles and high officials vied for the honor of manning the barge's towropes. A second barge carried Mut and Khonsu, the wife and son of Amen. All along the banks, the crowds watched and celebrated. By the time of Ramses III, this annual festival had stretched out to last almost a month.

Not all worship took place in the temples. Even in the poorest houses, there was usually a small shrine to a favorite god. There offerings would be made and prayers addressed. A wealthy noble might have his own elaborate chapel in a choice corner of his garden. The god honored in one of these private shrines was not necessarily a dominant figure of the pantheon, such as Amen-Re or Osiris. Bes, the squat, leopard-skin-clad god of the bedchamber, and Hathor, the goddess of love, were two favorites. Maybe as a natural result, another favorite was Taweret, a goddess in the form of a hippopotamus, who protected women during childbirth.

MUMMIES AND THE AFTERLIFE

The eager young archaeologist has been left alone with the expedition's most spectacular finds: an unusual mummy and a gold box with an elaborate curse engraved on its lid. He tries to concentrate on examining some broken tablets, but his attention keeps straying to the box. Finally, despite his superior's orders, he opens the box and finds a rolled papyrus. It is "the Scroll of Thoth, the great spell with which Isis raised Osiris from the dead." As he transcribes the hieroglyphs, he mouths the words. Behind him, we see the eyes of the mummy open a slit and the hands begin to move.

When the other members of the expedition return, they find the mummy case empty. The young man, laughing maniacally, points to the door and says, "He went for a little walk!"

This scene is from the 1932 movie *The Mummy,* starring Boris Karloff. It is still in the news over 60 years later; in 1997 an original poster for it sold at auction for over

$400,000. It was even featured on a recent U.S. postage stamp. This movie and its many imitators did a lot to shape our ideas about ancient Egypt. In particular, they spread the view that there is something inherently frightening about mummies. How many people would be eager to spend the night in the Egyptian collection of a museum? Even if they agreed to try it, how many would stay put after the first creaking noise that seemed to come from the direction of a nearby mummy case?

Death, and the possibility of somehow overcoming death, have preoccupied humankind for as long as we have any records. As part of this preoccupation, many cultures have tried to preserve the physical remains of their dead. The Incas of Peru kept the bodies of their dead kings in the Temple of the Sun, to be brought out on special occasions. Visitors to Assisi, in Italy, can still see the preserved body of Saint Clare, the 13th-century nun who worked closely with Saint Francis. In today's America, most people consider embalming to be an essential feature of the process of burial.

Nowhere has preserving the dead been as important, as widespread, as elaborate, and as effective as in ancient Egypt. This has given the culture the reputation of being morbidly fascinated by death, but this is not so. One of the most common oaths began "As I love life and hate death . . ." Egyptians appreciated life so much that they sought to do everything they could to prolong it *past* the moment of its end.

Fertile land has always been scarce in the Nile Valley, and the desert just a stone's throw away. These two facts shaped the burial customs of the culture. Since earliest times, the dead have been buried out a little beyond the limits of cultivation. In the predynastic era (about 5000–3200 BC), most graves were simple pits dug in the hot, dry sand. The dead person was usually placed on the left side, perhaps lying on a reed mat, with the knees drawn up and the face toward the west, the land of the setting sun. Often, painted pots, figurines, weapons, and pieces of carved ivory were put in the grave, too.

When a dead body is buried in hot, dry sand, an odd thing sometimes happens. Before the corpse has time to begin to rot, the surrounding sand draws all the moisture out of it. No moisture, no decay. The result is a natural mummy. This must have happened a great many times in predynastic Egypt. Often, too, shifting sand or the digging of an animal must have brought such a mummified body into sight.

The existence of these natural mummies probably helped shape the culture's beliefs about an afterlife. It must also have given people of the time the idea that the physical body could be preserved and taken into that other world. In response, they began to build elaborate stone-lined tombs and use wooden coffins to protect their chiefs and other important dead. Ironically, though, boxing in the body had the effect of keeping it away from the dry sand that might have preserved it. The fancier the burial, the less likely that the body would last.

If nature could not be counted on to turn a body into a mummy, then people would have to find ways to do it themselves. The first tries at mummification date to the time of the 1st dynasty, around 3000 BC. However, these early measures were not very effective at preserving the physical appearance of the body. Step by step, the embalmers invented new techniques. By the time of the pyramids, some 400 years later, all the basic steps of mummification were in use. Further improvements continued for hundreds of years. The embalmer's art reached its peak in Egypt toward the end of the New Kingdom, around 1000 BC.

HOW TO MAKE A MUMMY

How do you preserve a dead body against decaying and turning to dust? There are ways. Those who are unlucky enough to be swallowed up by one of the peat bogs of northern Europe are often mummified by a combination of high acidity and the absence of oxygen. Here and there in the world, there are grottoes where the mineral deposits in the walls turn those buried there into mummies; one well-known example is in Guanajuato, in central Mexico. Five hundred years ago, the Incas of Peru used a process a bit like modern freeze-drying to achieve a similar effect. Today, morticians rely on injecting preservative fluids into the body. But few would dispute that the all-time champions at preserving the dead for a very long time in something that approaches a lifelike state were the Egyptians, and particularly those of the 21st dynasty (1069–945 BC).

The method they used involved three critical steps: removing the soft parts of the body, which are especially likely to decay; eliminating moisture from the rest of the body; and protecting the desiccated remains.

After a ritual cleansing, the body was carried to a temporary workshop and laid out on a wooden table. One of the priests made a cut along the left side with a flint knife. Then, because he had damaged the body, the others ritually chased him away with shouted insults. They scraped out all the internal organs except the heart, which was considered the organ of thinking as well as feeling. That was left in place. The other organs were dried separately, then either preserved in special receptacles called canopic jars, or, less often, wrapped in linen and later put back inside the body cavity. The brain was removed with a long metal hook pushed through the thin ethmoid bone at the top of the nostril.

Now the eviscerated body was laid on a bed of natron, a

natural salt that is found in the Wadi Natrun northwest of Cairo. Natron, made up mostly of sodium carbonate and sodium bicarbonate, is a powerful drying agent. After filling the abdominal cavity with the substance, the priests covered the entire body with natron and left it to dry for forty days.

For a long time people believed that the body was soaked for forty days in a liquid solution of natron. The reason is that the Greek historian Herodotus, who wrote the earliest surviving description of the process, used a word that was later translated as "pickled." This gave rise to those horrific images in books and movies of corpses being lowered into huge steaming vats. It turns out that the word usually referred to the process of dry-salting fish. This was as close as Herodotus could come in Greek to the concept of mummification. Twenty-five hundred years later, a boatload of royal mummies being transported to the National Museum arrived in Cairo. The customs agent had to fill out an official declaration on the shipment. He scratched his head awhile, then classified it as *farseekh*—dried fish.

Once the body was thoroughly dry, it was ritually washed in water from the Nile, to flush away any natron that still clung to it. The skin now hung loose on the shrunken body. By the 21st dynasty, it was usual to soften it with oils and unguents, then pad it out with sawdust, mud, or cloth, to give it a more lifelike appearance. Sometimes the packers overdid it. The mummy of one queen, Nodjmet, looks as if her cheeks are overcrammed with walnuts.

Now the wrapping began, with long, narrow strips of linen. For a pharaoh or other important figure, the finest linen might be specially woven for the purpose. Others had to make do with whatever the family had around—old sheets, worn clothing, or even, in one case, a threadbare boat sail. After the head was tied in place, the fingers and toes—and, for males, the genitals—were individually wrapped.

Next came the arms and legs, then the torso. Once the first layer of wrapping was complete, it was brushed with hot liquid resins that later dried to a hard, almost glassy surface. Then another layer was added . . . and another, and another, in an order prescribed by ritual. In all, as many as 450 square yards (375 square meters) of linen might be needed to finish the job.

Once the wrapping was done, a mask was usually placed over the head and shoulders of the mummy. For most people, these masks were made of linen stiffened with plaster, painted to resemble a face. For a pharaoh, only gold would do. The gold mask of Tutankhamen, inlaid with semiprecious stones, is probably the most famous single object ever found in Egypt. Later, during the Roman period, wealthy people had their portraits painted while they were still alive, in encaustic—colored wax—on thin boards. After death, these amazingly realistic portraits were cut to size, placed over the face of the mummy, and fastened in place by the last layers of linen strips.

It is easy to slip into talking about mummification as a technical process—how did the Egyptians do it? This overlooks the crucial fact that mummification was a religious act. Those who carried it out had the status of priests. In tomb paintings the chief embalmer is shown in the form of the jackal-headed god, Anubis, protector of the dead. Carved Anubis masks with eyeholes under the jutting muzzle show that this was not just the painter's imagination at work.

At each stage of the process, particular amulets were placed on the mummy and particular prayers were said. These prayers and amulets were, in a sense, even more important than the mummification itself. With the correct prayers and amulets, even a badly prepared mummy could awaken to the other world, but if the rites were not properly carried out, even a perfectly preserved mummy would not be guaranteed a passage to the afterlife.

On the 70th day, the process was complete. The period of time had a religious significance. It represented the 70 days that the constellation Orion, the stellar home of Osiris, was hidden below the horizon before being reborn. Priests and mourners carried the mummified body in its coffin to the burial site. Servants brought along food and wine, flowers, furniture, clothing—whatever the dead person's spirit might need in the afterlife. For a soldier, there were weapons; for a scribe, brushes and blank scrolls; for a child, games and toys.

At the door of the tomb, the mummy was propped up in a standing position for a ceremony called "the Opening of the Mouth." A priest wearing the skin of a leopard touched different parts of the body with special instruments meant to restore the mummy's lost senses. The mouth was the most important. Once that had been restored, the mummy could magically take part in his or her own funeral feast, before being put to rest in the tomb. Even more crucial, the mummy would be able to recite all the proper spells on its journey to the afterlife.

The funeral was not the end. The next day, fresh offerings of food and drink were placed on a special table at the sealed door of the tomb. This continued for as long as the family kept it up. Those with enough money set up endowments, giving a fertile field to a local temple in return for daily offerings. However, these arrangements were like some of the "perpetual care" plans advertised by modern cemeteries. Sooner or later, they fell through. As insurance against that, farsighted Egyptians provided an alternative. On the inner walls of their tombs they painted lines of servants bearing trays of food and offering tables heaped high with good things. For the spirit, symbolic offerings were almost as good as the real thing.

THE JOURNEY TO THE OTHER WORLD

What beliefs led the Egyptians to place so much importance on the preservation of the body? The Western tradition is to distinguish between the body, the material self, and the soul, the spiritual self. It was not so simple in ancient Egypt. There were three different concepts that corresponded roughly to what would today be called the soul.

First, whenever the god Khnum shaped a new child on his potter's wheel, he also created a spiritual double of the child, called the *ka.* The *ka,* living on the spiritual plane, developed and changed as the person did, so in a sense it was what we would call the personality. After death, the physical person was reunited with his *ka,* which reanimated him and gave him strength.

Second, there was the *ba,* shown in tomb paintings as a human-headed bird equipped with a small lamp. The *ba*-bird, unlike the mummy that had given rise to it, could move around. It is often shown flying up the shaft of the tomb to the world of the living, to accept offerings and bring them back to the mummy.

Third, and most abstract, was the *akh,* sometimes translated as "transfigured spirit." This corresponded most closely to the modern concept of the soul. It was the *akh* that made the dangerous journey to the Duat, the world of the afterlife, with the help and protection of amulets and prayers that had been placed in the coffin and painted on the walls of the tomb.

The Egyptians were never quite in agreement on exactly where the other world might be located. Some said it was the underworld, where the sun disappeared on its nightly journey toward morning. Some claimed it was in the sky, among the stars. The west, where the sun dies each evening, and the east, where the sun is reborn each dawn, were also possibilities. Even the north, home of the only stars that never set, was mentioned.

Wherever the Duat was located, the sacred texts agreed that it was very much like Egypt, only better. It was warmed by constant sun and cooled by a pleasant north breeze. There the *akh* had a comfortable house and garden, nice things to wear, plenty to eat and drink, the comforting presence of loving family and friends, and freedom from the worries of earthly life.

As on earth, however, there was work to be done. Someone had to bake the bread, brew the beer, and do the laundry. But that was the job of the *ushabtis,* the little statues placed in such numbers in the tomb. The usual formula inscribed on them put it this way:

> *Thou ushabti! If I am called on to do any work that has to be done in the land of the dead—to fertilize the fields, to irrigate the banks, to carry sand from the east bank to the west bank—thou shalt say, "Here am I!"*

The Duat was a paradise . . . but first the *akh* had to get there. Demons and fierce animals lay in wait along the way. For each one, there was an amulet for protection and a magic spell to be said. It was not unusual for a mummy's wrappings to contain hundreds of different amulets. The most important of these was the heart scarab, made of lapis lazuli, carnelian, or other semiprecious stones and carved in the form of a beetle. A spell from the Book of the Dead was engraved on its bottom surface. Other spells were found on the sides of coffins and the walls of tombs and in papyrus scrolls placed in the coffin as a sort of guidebook for the *akh* on its journey.

If the *akh* managed to complete the voyage, Anubis, guardian of the dead, escorted it into the Hall of Judgment. There Osiris, ruler of the Duat, waited on his throne. In the center of the hall was an enormous pair of scales. Standing next to them was Thoth, the scribe of the gods, who served as a sort of court reporter. The person's heart was placed on one pan of the scales. On the other was placed a feather, symbol of Ma'at, the goddess of truth.

Crouched under the scales, watching hungrily, was a fearsome creature with a crocodile's jaws, a lion's forequarters, and a hippo's hindquarters. It was named, ominously, the Gobbler of Shadows. If the newcomer had done evil in life, his heart was heavier than Ma'at's feather, tipping the scales, and the Gobbler ate it. This time, death was forever. If the two scales balanced, however, the *akh* passed on into the Duat.

Naturally, for such an overwhelmingly important decision, there was an appropriate spell for the *akh* to recite. This was known as the Negative Confession. A small sample:

> *Homage to you, O ye gods who live in your hall of Right and Truth. I have come unto you; I have committed no faults; I have not sinned; I have done no evil . . . I have given bread unto the hungry and water unto those who thirst, clothing unto the naked, and a boat unto the shipwrecked mariner . . . O, then, deliver ye me and protect me; accuse me not before the great god . . .*

Historians are still arguing about the moral significance of the *akh*'s appearance before Osiris and the Court of Judgment. On one hand, the Negative Confession covers most of the "thou shalt nots" in the Ten Commandments and a good many other sins as well. Was this, as some have called it, the dawn of conscience? Maybe; but others point out that the Negative Confession is part of a book of magical spells. Its purpose may have been not to teach people what deeds to shun, but to magically wipe away deeds the person had already done. By this interpretation, the *akh* before Osiris was a little like a three-year-old standing next to the fragments of a broken vase and saying, "I didn't do it!"

And what of those—most people, surely—who could not afford to buy a handwritten scroll of the Book of the Dead for their coffin and could not have read it even if they had one? If they didn't know the correct formulas to recite, did that mean that the Gobbler of Shadows automatically got them? At this point, we have no way of knowing.

Putting Mummies to Use

The custom of mummifying the dead continued in Egypt from the time of the earliest pharaohs right through the Roman period, a time span of over three thousand years. It finally ended only with the rise of Christianity in Egypt. Even then, the memory of the custom remained, along with cemeteries and caves filled with many thousands of wrapped and embalmed bodies. Because the resins with which they were coated turned them black, they came to be called "mummies," from a Persian word, *mumia,* which means bitumen or pitch.

This name led to one of the more peculiar sidelights of Egyptian history. Persian physicians in medieval times claimed that *mumia*—that is, the mineral pitch sometimes found oozing from rocks in oil-rich regions—cured cuts, mended broken bones, and healed stomach ailments. The problem was that *mumia* was scarce and expensive. The blackened resins found on the outside and inside of mummies looked much the same, and the names *were* the same. So why not use those instead? Soon the bodies of long-dead Egyptians were being ground up and sold as medicine.

By the 16th century, "powdered mummy" was an important export of Egypt and a standard item at apothecary shops throughout Europe. The demand became so great that it eventually outran the supply. Some dealers found a profitable solution to this problem. They started manufacturing their own mummies. They bought fresh corpses from the prisons and hospitals, stuffed them with pitch, and wrapped them in old rags. After a few weeks of aging under the Egyptian sun, the new "mummies" were powdered and sold as the genuine article.

Eventually word of this scam spread. The news killed off the trade in mummies. Patients may have been ready to swallow the dust of people who had died 2,000 years before, but they drew the line at those who had died only a few months before, of who knew what loathsome disease.

Even after Europeans stopped taking mummies as medicine, however, they continued to collect them. No wealthy traveler making the Grand Tour could return home from Egypt without a stuffed crocodile to hang on the wall, a selection of scarabs and pots to display in a curio cabinet, and an occupied mummy case. Once home, some even invited friends over to watch the mummy being unwrapped. These mummies usually ended up in the basement of a local museum or disappeared altogether, along with whatever knowledge of ancient times they might have given us.

In the Victorian era, Thomas Cook began offering organized tours of Egypt and the Holy Land. A high point was a guided visit to a tomb where a mummy would be "found," then taken back to the hotel to be unrolled after dinner. Even if these excursions took place only every two weeks for only 20 years, they would have used up at least 500 mummies . . . because, of course, once unwrapped, the mummies were considered to be of no use to anyone.

Their fate could have been still worse. At one point in the 19th century, an American paper manufacturer signed a contract to buy tons of linen wrappings from mummies, to be made into rag-content paper. No mention was made of what would be done with the mummies themselves, but it is easy to imagine. The deal eventually fell through, after the rumor started that the paper could spread diseases from ancient times.

This widespread disrespect for the remains of the long-dead inspired Mark Twain, in his satirical travel book *The Innocents Abroad,* to describe an Egyptian train trip this way:

> *The fuel they use for the locomotives is composed of mummies three thousand years old, purchased by the ton or by the graveyard for that purpose. Sometimes one hears the profane engineer call out pettishly, "D——n these plebeians, they don't burn worth a cent—pass out a king."*

Scientists Look at Mummies

Not everyone treated mummies as mere curiosities. Beginning in the 19th century, scholars and scientists have tried to learn from them, using the most advanced tools available to them at the time. One of the first carefully detailed accounts of unwrapping a mummy was published in 1814 by Jacques-Joseph Champollion, whose younger brother, Jean-François, would later become one of the most important figures in the history of Egyptology. The most interesting feature of the mummy, a young man from the Ptolemaic period, was the gold toe and finger caps, which were still in place. After studying the mummy, the Champollion brothers rewrapped it (not very well). It is now one of seven human mummies in the museum of Grenoble, France.

In 1881 a remarkable cache of mummies from the New Kingdom was unearthed near Deir el Bahri and removed to the Cairo Museum. The museum staff, under the direction of Sir Gaston Maspero, head of the museum, unwrapped many of the mummies soon after their arrival. One of these was Thutmose III (1504–1450 BC), victor of the battle of Megiddo and stepson of the female pharaoh Hatshepsut. Grave robbers had left him in terrible shape, slashing through the wrappings in search of jewels and amulets. When the linen tapes were removed, Maspero found that the head and legs of the pharaoh had been ripped from his body. Reassembling the body, he discovered that the great general, who had created an empire stretching from the Sudan to the borders of Turkey, was barely five feet tall.

It was several years before Maspero unwrapped another royal mummy. This time he chose Ramses II, renowned for his long reign, many wives, and fondness for building grandiose monuments to himself. To Maspero's relief, the mummy of Ramses was perfectly preserved. Not so the next one unwrapped, that of queen Ahmose Nefertari. As Maspero wrote, "the body was no sooner exposed to the outer air than it fell literally into a state of putrefaction, dissolving into black matter which gave out an insupportable smell."

In 1895 a German scientist, Wilhelm Roentgen, startled the world with a photograph of his wife's hand in which the bones showed plainly while the flesh was only faint shadows. He had made this photograph using a form of radiation he had discovered and named *X rays*. Egyptologists quickly realized that this discovery meant they could examine mummies in great detail without damaging or even unwrapping them. The first X-ray pictures of mummies were made within a few years of Roentgen's discovery. Still, it was not until the 1960s that scholars were finally given permission to X-ray the royal mummies in the Cairo Museum. Among their discoveries was that Ramses II had painful dental problems that included badly worn-down back teeth, abscessed teeth, and diseased gums.

Today, museums throughout the world have X-rayed the mummies in their collections, yielding a wealth of information about their age, body structure, family resemblances, and illnesses. Sometimes there are surprises, too. One mummy had an extra skull tucked inside its wrappings. Another turned out to be a collection of miscellaneous bones.

In recent years, new technologies have arrived on the scene. Using computerized axial tomography (a "CAT scan"), radiologists can create a three-dimensional picture of a mummy that shows not only the bones but softer tissues as well. Endoscopes, fiber-optic viewing devices hardly thicker than a thread, allow investigators to look around *inside* a mummy without damaging it. More experimental techniques for examining the genetic structure of cells may soon tell us the names and family relationships of mummies whose identity is still a mystery.

The Other Mummies

About halfway between Cairo and Luxor, on the west bank of the Nile, is an ancient city of the dead called Tuna el-Gebel. The catacombs under it contain at least four million mummies, perhaps as many as eight million. But these are not pharaohs, or even peasants. They are ibises and baboons. These two creatures were sacred to the god Thoth, who had an important temple here. The temple raised flocks of birds and troops of apes. Anyone who sought the god's favor could pay to have an animal sacrificed and mummified, then entombed in one of the labyrinthine underground passages.

At one time or another, the Egyptians mummified almost every sort of animal to be found in their land: snakes and rats, dogs and lizards, rams and gazelles, and every variety of bird. Most were deliberately sacrificed to a particular god, like the baboons and ibises dear to Thoth. Falcons were dedicated to Horus, the falcon-headed son of Osiris and Isis. Crocodiles were sacred to Sobek, and jackals to Anubis. Cats symbolized the goddess Bast. Although many cats that were mummified were probably favorite pets that had died a natural death, others had clearly been sacrificed.

The most important of the animal cults was that of the Apis bull. From time to time, a black calf was born with a white diamond on its forehead and the outline of eagle wings on its back. These were the signs of an Apis bull, the god Ptah come down to earth, and the whole kingdom rejoiced. An Apis bull was tended carefully its whole life. When one died, its body was mummified and entombed at Memphis. The sarcophagus, as big as a small room, was carved from a single block of granite or limestone, and there was space in the underground complex for at least 28 such burials.

Later, during the Ptolemaic period, Apis became identified with Osiris, and the two names, Osiris and Apis, merged to become Serapis. The chief temple of Serapis was one of the great monuments of Alexandria until 391 AD, when the Roman emperor Theodosius ordered it leveled to the ground.

PART II

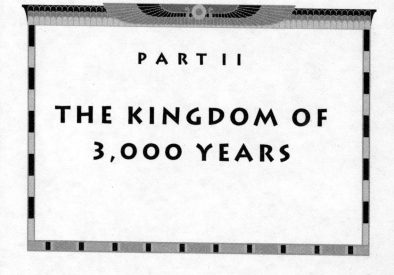

THE KINGDOM OF 3,000 YEARS

THE GROWTH OF A GREAT POWER

Historians sometimes argue among themselves about events that took place only a few years ago, or a few dozen years ago. Exactly what happened, and exactly when did it happen? Even with billions of pages of archives and the testimony of eyewitnesses, the answers are not always obvious or clear-cut. Imagine, then, how much harder it is to be definite about anything that happened over five thousand years ago, at a time when the art of writing was still almost unknown. Put in this light, it is amazing that we know as much about the beginnings of Egyptian civilization as we do.

One important thing we *don't* know for sure is how it began. We have already seen how the Nile Valley was settled. We have seen how its unique features encouraged the development of agriculture, the settling of villages and towns, the construction of canals and dikes, and the growth of trade up and down the river. All these developments took place gradually, step by step, over many centuries.

Toward the end of the 4th millennium BC, however, Egyptian culture seemed to transform itself with astonishing speed. In a relatively short time there appeared a sophisticated system of writing and an increasingly centralized government that was capable of directing huge, highly organized building projects like nothing the earth had seen before. The change is so dramatic that some people find it impossible to believe ordinary humans could have carried it out. They insist that the credit must belong to a caste of wise men from drowned Atlantis, or perhaps to a caste of wise aliens from another star system.

The most likely explanation is much more everyday, though still amazing. In place of mysterious white-robed figures with enormous eyes and no ears, imagine a marketplace in one of the coastal towns in the Delta. A trader from farther up the coast, from Phoenicia or Syria, has just concluded a bargain. He takes out a moist clay tablet and a stick with a wedge-shaped point and makes some marks in the clay. When his Egyptian counterpart asks what he is doing, he says, "It's a new way of keeping track of our deal. A buddy of mine learned about it a few months back when he was in Sumer. And by the way, he was telling me about some of the temples they've started putting up there. You wouldn't believe it. They practically reach to the sky!"

Later, the Egyptian merchant passes along this interesting information to a friend from upriver who is a priest or a court official. The friend has been wrestling with the problem of keeping track of religious festivals or taxes paid. In the cartoon bubble over the friend's head, we see a lightbulb (or in this case, an oil lamp) go on. The next day, he starts making his own marks with a stick of charcoal on a broken piece of pottery.

Archaeologists and anthropologists call this process *stimulus diffusion.* Objects found in graves of the predynastic era show that Egyptians were in contact with the Sumerian culture in Mesopotamia, at a time when the Sumerians were developing the beginnings of both writing and monumental architecture. What is confusing is that the Egyptians did not copy the Sumerians directly. The little symbols called hieroglyphs, drawn on papyrus sheets, do not look a bit like the wedge-shaped marks of cuneiform pressed into clay tablets. A pyramid does not resemble a round ziggurat with its spiral ramp rising to the top. Instead, what the Egyptians apparently took from the Sumerians were the *ideas* of writing and of building massively. Once they had these ideas firmly in mind, they went on to carry them out in their own ways.

At the early stages of this process, Egyptians did some fairly direct borrowing, too. This is one reason the stimulus diffusion theory is considered more solidly based than other explanations. For example, the ziggurats of Mesopotamia were built of mud brick, because good building stone was scarce in that part of the world. In Egypt there was plenty of stone, easily available, yet the earliest big buildings were constructed of mud brick. Some even had architectural features that were typically Mesopotamian. And when Egyptians did begin to build in stone, at first they cut their stones to the size of a Mesopotamian mud brick instead of the larger blocks they used later.

Another example: To seal a container or door, Sumerians used hard cylinders engraved with cuneiform. These were rolled across a lump of soft clay or wax to form the seal. Under the pharaohs, for the same purpose, Egyptians used scarab stamps with hieroglyphs carved into their underside. However, some *Egyptian* cylinder seals have been found from the era just before the pharaohs. We know they are Egyptian, and not imports from Sumeria, because instead of cuneiform, they are engraved with little pictures that are clearly the ancestors of hieroglyphs.

A Record of the Past

In 285 BC, Ptolemy II, who was of Greek origin and a descendant of one of Alexander the Great's generals, assumed the title of pharaoh. Apparently he was eager to learn about the past of his new kingdom. He asked the high priest at Heliopolis to write him a history of Egypt. The priest, Manetho, a native of the Delta town of Sebenithe, was in a superb position to do this. The temple of the sun god Re had detailed historical records that went back as much as two thousand years.

Manetho structured his history around the concept of a *dynasty,* a series of kings who were related to each other. He listed 31 of them, from the unification of Upper and Lower Egypt, around 3100 BC, to the victory of Alexander the Great in 332 BC. It is not always obvious why Manetho placed a particular pharaoh at the end of one dynasty rather than the beginning of the next one. It is not even clear why he broke up certain historical periods into several different dynasties.

These questions might be easier to answer if we had a copy of Manetho's book. Unfortunately, none has survived. All we have of it are some passages quoted by much later authors, who had their own points to prove, and some badly garbled lists of kings and dates copied from it. Even so, with a lot of corrections from what archaeology has uncovered, Manetho's work is still the essential framework on which our knowledge of Egyptian history is built.

We have other sources, but they, too, are incomplete. One notable example is the Turin Papyrus, which dates from the reign of Ramses II and gives a list of all his predecessors (or at least, the ones he approved of). It was found in AD 1823 by Bernadino Drovetti. Drovetti was French consul to Egypt and had a great deal of power and influence. He used his position ruthlessly to amass huge numbers of valuable antiquities that he later sold to major collectors in Europe. Supposedly the Turin Papyrus was in one piece when Drovetti acquired it. He then carried it to Cairo on donkeyback. By the time he arrived, the fragile scroll had crumbled into hundreds of tiny, thoroughly mixed up fragments. Scholars have been trying to fit the pieces back together, and cursing Drovetti's name, ever since.

Another record, this time of the five earliest dynasties, was carved on stone. This, too, is now in fragments. The largest piece found is in the museum of Palermo, Italy. Other bits, or bits of copies, are in museums in London and Cairo.

One improvement that modern Egyptologists have made to Manetho's list of dynasties is to group them into larger time spans that reflect different cultural and historical patterns. These are:

DYNASTY	PERIOD	APPROXIMATE DATES (BC)
1st–2nd	Archaic	3150–2686
3rd–6th	Old Kingdom	2686–2181
7th–10th	1st Intermediate	2181–2040
11th–13th	Middle Kingdom	2040–1782
14th–17th	2nd Intermediate	1782–1570
18th–20th	New Kingdom	1570–1070
21st–31st	3rd Intermediate	1069–525
	"Late"	525–332
	Greek	332–30

More details can be found in the time line at the beginning of the book.

The reason these dates are approximate (and a nagging source of disagreement among experts) is that unlike, say, the Romans, who dated events from the legendary founding of Rome, the Egyptians did not number their years from any single starting point. Instead, they usually dated events by referring to a particular year in the reign of a certain pharaoh or to some memorable event ("In the second year after the campaign in Nubia"). In most cases, we do not even know exactly how long the various pharaohs held the throne. Our best estimates are based on such things as noticing that there are records of events dated to Year 17 of a particular pharaoh, but none for Year 18. These facts make it reasonable to assume that his reign lasted only 17 years.

To make the question of dates even more confusing, there were periods in which the reigns of two pharaohs overlapped, either because one was sharing the title with his heir or because there were competing centers of power. In these cases, some events might be dated to Year so-and-so of one pharaoh, while other events that took place at exactly the same time were dated to a different year of the other pharaoh.

Difficult as it is, however, the situation is not impossible. A few records fix certain astronomical events as taking place on a particular date of a certain year in the reign of a certain pharaoh. From that, and our knowledge of astronomy, modern scholars can determine the exact year, then work backward and forward from that fixed point.

Here is an example. In predynastic times, Egyptians noticed that the first dawn appearance of the star Sirius after its absence from the sky—what is called its *heliacal rising*—occurred just before the annual Nile flood began. This struck them as so significant that they made it the starting point for their calendar. However, because the calendar did not include a leap year, it gradually drifted out of synch with the stars. So when scholars found a mention that Sirius rose on a particular date in Year Seven of the reign of Middle Kingdom pharaoh Senwosret III, a simple calculation showed that this corresponded to 1872 BC. A different dated reference to the heliacal rising of Sirius, this one from the reign of Amenhotep I, is not quite as useful. Because we do not know whether the observation was made at Thebes or at Heliopolis, 450 miles farther north, all it tells us is that it took place at some point within a 26-year time span, but not exactly when.

CONQUEST AND UNITY

In his chronicle, Manetho tells of a mighty warrior named Scorpion who ruled a kingdom in Upper Egypt, near the First Cataract, around 3150 BC. Scorpion made war on his neighbors to the north and eventually expanded his kingdom to include all the Nile Valley as far as present-day Cairo. His successor, Menes, went on to conquer the Delta region. For the first time, all of Egypt was united under the rule of one king. Menes then shrewdly built a new capital city, Memphis, on the border between Upper and Lower Egypt

All the ancient king lists agree that Menes was the first pharaoh and founder of Egypt. Modern experts were inclined to think of Menes as a mythical figure, along the lines of Romulus and Remus or King Arthur. Then a magnificent carved slate palette turned up in the ruins of a temple at Hierakonpolis, between Thebes and the First Cataract. It is now one of the great treasures of the Cairo Museum.

On one side, the palette shows a kilted king wearing the

White Crown of Upper Egypt. He is about to bash open the head of a kneeling enemy. Above the victim, a falcon leads a human-headed papyrus boat. This means approximately, "Falcon-headed Horus gives the captive Delta to the King." On the other side, the same king is now wearing the Red Crown of Lower Egypt as he inspects a battlefield with rows of fallen warriors. The central design is two lions with very long, entwined necks. These may stand for unity. At the top of the slate, on both sides, is a rectangular frame that contains the name of the king: Narmer.

The meaning is clear: King Narmer, originally from Upper Egypt, won a great victory over the warriors of Lower Egypt and unified the country under his rule. But who was Narmer? Why didn't he appear on the king lists? Above all, why did he apparently carry out the deeds traditionally credited to Menes? One obvious possibility, which many experts support, is that Menes and Narmer are two names for the same person. Pharaohs traditionally had several official names. Maybe the one inscribed on the palette simply did not make its way into the records that Manetho and others consulted almost 3,000 years later.

Whatever the case, Menes and his successors of the 1st and 2nd dynasties did everything they could to unify the country while recognizing regional differences. The White Crown of Upper Egypt and the Red Crown of Lower Egypt were merged—awkwardly—to form the Double Crown. Royal palaces were always built with two main entrances, the Gate of the North and the Gate of the South. Even the pharaoh's titles reflected this concern. He was never king of Egypt, but always Lord of the Two Lands, King of Upper and Lower Egypt, Beloved of the Two Ladies (the great goddesses of the two regions). One even put on his seal the animals that represented both the ancient enemies, Horus and Set.

The pharaohs of the Archaic Period accomplished many things. They built Memphis into a major city. They increased the amount of land that could be farmed by adding to the system of irrigation and by reclaiming swamp and marshland. They encouraged foreign trade, importing cedar logs from Phoenicia and ebony and ivory from central Africa. They assembled armies of officials and scribes to carry on the business of an increasingly powerful centralized government. They built elaborate tombs for themselves, either at Saqqâra, near Memphis, or at Abydos, the holy city of Osiris. In fact, some built themselves tombs in *both* places, to the great confusion of archaeologists later on. (Presumably they only occupied one of them.) However, it was left for those who came after them, the pharaohs of the Old Kingdom, to make the astonishing leap that would imprint an image of Egypt indelibly on the consciousness of humankind.

THE FIRST GENIUS

Imhotep was the vizier, or chancellor, of pharaoh Djoser (around 2668–2649 BC). Later generations deified Imhotep and said that he was the son of Thoth, the god who invented writing and numbers. They called him Egypt's first great astronomer, architect, physician, and sage, and said that he was the first person ever to build large structures of dressed, squared-off stone. According to the evidence, it seems quite possible that in this, at the very least, they were right.

Until Djoser's time, pharaohs and other important figures were buried in hidden chambers at the bottom of deep shafts in the rock, which could be filled in for security after the burial. Covering the top of the shaft was a rectangular building made of mud brick that contained chapels, storerooms, and halls where visitors could bring offerings. As these buildings decayed over many centuries, they came to look like the mud brick benches called *mastabas* that are a common feature of Arab villages, so they began to be called that.

A pharaoh's tomb was called a House of Eternity. It was meant to last forever. Of course, even the grandest structure made of mud brick eventually decays to a mere mound of dirt.

Djoser apparently wanted a more impressive fate for his eternal home. He got it. As his architect, Imhotep had the inspiration to build a huge mastaba, not of mud brick but of stone, then to build another, slightly smaller, on top of it. This in turn was topped by two more in diminishing sizes. As he was building it, Imhotep decided to make the structure still bigger. He expanded the already completed layers on two sides, then put two more layers on top of them. Once completed, it was by far the largest building on earth at the time, known as the Step Pyramid. Its distinctive outline reflected its spiritual function as a staircase for the king to mount to the sky after death.

Imhotep's achievement on behalf of pharaoh Djoser was the earliest moment in what came to be called the Age of Pyramids. For the next two centuries, one pharaoh after another commanded his own imposing House of Eternity. Some were never finished, and can now be traced only as outlines in the sand. Others were finished but apparently never used. One pharaoh, Snefru, built *two* pyramids, each larger than Djoser's. But it was Snefru's son, Khufu (better known as Cheops, the name the Greeks later called him), who brought the Age of Pyramids to its highest point. On the plateau of Giza, north of Memphis, he built a structure that is still one of the wonders of the world: the Great Pyramid. Its history and mysteries are told in detail in Chapter 8.

Seventy-five years ago, a photographer was setting up his

equipment to take a photograph of Khufu's pyramid. One of the feet of his tripod made a nick in a layer of plaster that for 4,500 years had concealed the top of a shaft dug into the rock. American archaeologist George Reisner and his team began clearing out the shaft. A hundred feet down, they found a small, rough tomb choked with a jumble of broken furniture, alabaster and gold jars, boxes, baskets, and chests. Against one wall, piled high with what turned out to be a dismantled bed canopy, was a massive alabaster sarcophagus. Its heavy lid was still in place. The hieroglyphs on a scrap of gold leaf identified its owner: Queen Hetepheres, wife of Snefru and mother of Khufu.

Reisner was one of the most meticulous archaeologists of the 20th century. He and his team spent the next two years removing the contents of the tomb, piece by tiny piece. The furniture, inlaid with ebony and gold leaf, had decayed and collapsed, but they photographed and sketched the position of each fragment with such care and accuracy that restorers were later able to reconstruct the most important pieces. These include a slanting bed with inlaid footboard, one of the half-moon-shaped headrests that Egyptians used instead of pillows, and a chair with the queen's titles carved in hieroglyphs so detailed that every feather can be made out on the tiny bird symbols.

At last, in 1928, the burial chamber was clear, except for the sarcophagus itself. An eager group of distinguished visitors made their way down to the tomb. Workers levered up the massive lid, and Reisner looked inside.

Wherever Hetepheres might have been, she was not there. The sarcophagus was empty.

Eventually Reisner came up with an explanation for her absence. He suggested that she had originally been buried in one of her husband Snefru's two pyramids at Dahshur, south of Giza. Then robbers managed to penetrate her tomb and stole her mummy to get at the many jeweled amulets wrapped with it. The official in charge of the royal tombs could hardly admit to Khufu that his royal mother's body was lost forever. For such a crime, the best he could hope for would have been a quick death instead of a lingering one. So he faked it. He reburied the queen's sarcophagus and her funerary possessions in a hastily dug tomb at Giza. Presumably Khufu never knew that his mother's sarcophagus was now empty.

Not everyone accepts Reisner's theory. Other royal coffins, still sealed after thousands of years, have turned out to be empty. One even had a withered funeral wreath still resting on the lid. Were these vacant sarcophagi meant as decoys, in a last line of defense against tomb robbers? Were the bodies actually buried elsewhere, for some religious or magical reason? It is at least possible that somewhere in Giza or elsewhere, there is an undiscovered vault that still shelters the mummy of Queen Hetepheres.

The Door of the South

Most of the stone blocks used to construct the pyramids came from quarries right on the Giza plateau or, for the fine white limestone used for casing stones, from Tura, across the Nile. The harder, more durable red granite used for statues and burial chambers had to come all the way from Aswan, 400 miles upriver. Aswan and the nearby island of Elephantine, in the middle of the Nile, marked the border between Egypt and Nubia.

In later centuries Nubia became a province of Egypt, but during the Old Kingdom it was still a mysterious land. It was the source of precious goods—gold, ivory, ebony, ostrich feathers. It was also the home of fierce warriors who occasionally preyed on traders or even strayed across the border into Egypt. To control these far-off menaces, the pharaohs relied on deputies stationed at Elephantine.

These "Lords of the Door of the South" had a great deal of power and discretion. We know their names and histories, because they had their biographies inscribed on the walls of their tombs. Instead of seeking to be buried near the tomb of their pharaoh, as had been the custom in the past, they cut their tombs into the cliffs on the western bank of the river across from Elephantine. This is one of the first ominous signs of a localizing trend that would later tear the kingdom apart.

One of the early commanders at Elephantine was named Harkhuf. He made four major expeditions south into the Sudan, the first one when he was still a boy. The fourth expedition took place early in the reign of Pepi II, who took the throne when he was just five or six. On his return, Harkhuf reported to the pharaoh that he had brought back, not only gold and other rich goods, but also a dancing Pygmy.

The child pharaoh was thrilled. He immediately sent a reply to Harkhuf. It must have been written on papyrus, but later Harkhuf transcribed it onto the wall of his tomb. "You tell me that you have brought a Pygmy from the land of spirits," Pepi II wrote. "Hurry and bring northward with you to the Court this Pygmy to delight the heart. When he goes down with you into the ship, get trustworthy people to stay beside him on the deck, lest he fall into the water. When he sleeps at night, get trustworthy people to sleep beside him in his tent. Inspect him ten times a night! For My Majesty wants to see this Pygmy more than all the products of Sinai and Punt!"

Pepi II went on to rule as pharaoh for more than 90 years, the longest reign recorded in all the three millennia of

Egyptian history. Unfortunately, this was not to be his only distinction. He was also the last real ruler of the Old Kingdom. After his death around 2184, the country fell apart. Local strongmen took over and quarreled with each other. Some proclaimed themselves pharaoh, but no one else paid much attention to this. It was said of the 7th and 8th dynasties that they consisted of 70 kings in 70 days. Like many exaggerations, this contained an element of truth. In fact, these two "dynasties" probably lasted a total of no more than 25 years and had hardly any power even then.

The dissolution of the kingdom had been long in coming. In theory the pharaoh as god-king was the owner of everything in Egypt. He granted estates to important officials and favorites, but it was understood that these came back to the crown when a noble died. As the years went on, however, more and more nobles proclaimed that these lands were theirs by right and could be passed on to their children. They began to call themselves *erapti-hati-a,* "hereditary princes." Great estates grew up along the banks of the Nile, the property of the same noble families from generation to generation. With these independent sources of wealth and power, the nobles began to pay less attention to the central government.

During this same period, the priesthood also grew in power and influence. One pharaoh after another gave lands, riches, and slaves to the temples to support their religious activities. Over generations, this wealth accumulated. Then at the beginning of the 5th dynasty (around 2498 BC), the priesthood of Re, the sun god, whose great temple at Heliopolis harbored the *benben*—a conical stone that was the holiest object in Egypt—put forth a new claim. Pharaoh was not so much Horus, a god in his own right, they said, as the son of Re. That meant, of course, that he should pay particular attention to the advice of his divine father's priests and be particularly generous to his temples.

The erosion and eventual breakdown of the central power led to disorder on a more personal scale, too. "Indeed, the land spins round like a potter's wheel. The robber is now the possessor of riches and the rich man has become a plunderer . . . Indeed, the ship of state has broken up; towns are destroyed, and Upper Egypt has become an empty waste . . . Indeed, laughter has perished . . . It is groaning that is throughout the land, mingled with complaints." This powerful description comes from a sage named Ipuwer, whose writings continued to be copied and studied for centuries after his time.

Another prophet from the same period, Neferti, lamented that "this land is destroyed and there are none who care for it . . . Wild beasts of the desert will drink from the river of Egypt, taking their ease on the riverbanks through lack of anyone to fear . . . I show you the son as a foe, the brother as an enemy, a man killing his own father . . . Men take a man's property away from him and give it to outsiders."

Even the dead were not safe: "The gods who lived formerly rested in their pyramids; the beatified dead also, buried in their pyramids, and they who built houses [of Eternity—that is, tombs]—their places are no more. I have heard the words of Imhotep and Hordedef, with whose discourses men speak so much; what are their places now? Their walls are broken apart, and their places are no more, as though they had never been."

This period of disorder lasted about 140 years. In the context of the 3,000-year history of Egypt, that may not sound like much. For the people who lived through parts of it, it must have felt like forever. By way of comparison, it is about the same length of time as from the beginning of the American Civil War to the present.

Just as the rule of the pharaohs collapsed gradually, so it was gradually reestablished. A powerful family from the Faiyum, a rich, fertile region west of the Nile, established a new capital at Herakleopolis. They expanded their control to include the Delta and much of the Nile Valley and began to call themselves pharaohs. Manetho later referred to them as the 9th and 10th dynasties. Trade began to revive, the arts flourished, and the army grew strong enough to push foreign intruders out of the frontier regions. It must have seemed as if Herakleopolis was destined to lead the rebirth of Egypt.

However, the rule of these pharaohs did not extend farther upriver than the holy city of Abydos. All the territory beyond that was ruled by the prince of a rising city called Thebes. A century before, Thebes had been little more than a small river town, known mainly for its devotion to the war god, Montu, and its temple to another, more mysterious god named Amen. As the central power declined, Thebes took over the important trade with Nubia and the lands farther south. The town grew steadily in size, wealth, and influence. Soon its princes declared their independence from Herakleopolis and started to call themselves kings.

In 2060 BC a man named Mentuhotep became ruler of Thebes. After several years of hard fighting, he besieged and captured Herakleopolis. Egypt was once more united under a single conquering pharaoh, and once more that conquerer had come from the South. Mentuhotep went on to rule for over half a century. He was followed on the throne by two other members of his family. On the death of Mentuhotep III, his vizier, Amenemhet, took power and founded the 12th dynasty, which ruled ably for over 200 years.

The rulers of the 12th dynasty—almost all named either

Amenemhet or Senwosret—extended Egyptian rule southward into Nubia and the Sudan, pushed back Libyan raiders to the west, and built a line of fortifications in the Sinai to protect the rich mines there and the trade routes with Asia. The Egyptian objects from this period found in Lebanon, Syria, and Crete show that foreign trade was flourishing. However, one of the most important achievements of this period was domestic.

The Faiyum is a large depression in the desert west of the Nile, linked to the river by a narrow stream bed and by subterranean water tables. In prehistoric times it had been a large lake. By the time of the 12th dynasty, it was mostly seasonal pools and marshland, known for its immense flocks of migratory water birds. Amenemhet III, however, undertook a vast project of water control, irrigation, and land reclamation that included a retaining wall over 25 miles long. In a land where every bit of arable land is cherished, the project added as much as 27,000 acres to Egypt's stock of farmland. Since all this new land belonged to the crown, the project also added greatly to the wealth of the pharaoh.

Like Mentuhotep, the first pharaoh of the Middle Kingdom, Amenemhet III reigned for half a century. This was to be a high point of the period. After him, there was another slow decline that may have been caused in part by climatic changes. The Nile floods were irregular and followed by poor harvests. In the minds of the people, one of the most important functions of the pharaoh was to make sure the Nile behaved properly, so these bad years must have hurt the prestige and power of the throne. New pharaohs came and went quickly, leaving few records or accomplishments behind.

Still, the bureaucracy set up by the 12th-dynasty pharaohs continued to function. Trade with Phoenicia and Syria went on. New temples, tombs, and towns were built, even if the standards of art and craft were not quite what they had been. The kingdom was still united and its different regions at peace with one another. It might well have recovered from its problems, if it had not suddenly been attacked from without.

GLORY DAYS

In the reign of Tutimaois, it came to pass, I know not why, that a blast of God smote us, and unexpectedly, from the lands of the East, invaders of obscure race marched in confidence of victory against our land. They easily seized it by force without a battle. And when they had overpowered our rulers, they then burned our cities ruthlessly, razed the temples of the gods, and treated all the inhabitants with cruel hostility, for they slew some and led the children and wives of others into slavery . . . Finally, they appointed as king one of their number . . . All this nation was called Hyksos, that is, Shepherd Kings; for "hyk" in the sacred language denotes a king, and "sos" in the vulgar tongue signifies a shepherd.

This is one of the few passages from Manetho's history book that has come down to us. It is not entirely accurate; the name "Hyksos" actually came from the Egyptian *heka-khasut,* meaning "rulers of foreign lands," and the invasion does not seem to have been either as brutal or as sudden as he portrays it. Still, there *was* a successful invasion and conquest of Egypt in about 1660 BC, by a foreign people who came from the East, probably from Palestine or Syria. Manetho was writing about it 13 centuries later, so any inaccuracies are understandable, even though he must have had access to records that have since been lost.

At the time of the Hyksos invasion, Semitic people from Palestine had been drifting into the Delta region for hundreds of years. Some were traders, others were herders and farmers trying to find a haven from drought and famine. The Bible story of Joseph, who was sold into slavery in Egypt, may be an echo of how still others arrived. By the later years of the Middle Kingdom, there were many Asiatics in the Delta and in Upper Egypt, working as cooks, seamstresses, vineyard workers, and even temple dancers. As their children assimilated and took Egyptian names, their presence became unremarked and untraceable.

The arrival of the Hyksos was different. It was not a casual, gradual infiltration, but the migration of a whole people. More ominous, the invaders had a large, well-organized army. The pharaohs, secure behind the barrier of the Eastern and Western Deserts, had never felt the need for such an institution. Egyptian armies had always been drafted whenever needed, then disbanded after a crisis passed.

The invaders also had two powerful secret weapons that had been developed in Asia Minor. The first was the horse-drawn chariot. This would come to dominate the ancient battlefield as completely as the armored tank was to do in our own era. Egyptian warriors, who always fought on foot, had never seen anything like the charge of a company of chariots. They could not stand against it. Second, the Hyksos used recurved compound bows of wood, sinew, and horn. These were far more powerful and had a much longer range than the simple bows of the Egyptians. With superiority in arms, numbers, and organization, it is no wonder that the Hyksos "marched in confidence of victory." Their confidence was justified by the outcome.

Once in control, the invaders established their capital at Avaris, in the eastern part of the Delta. Then they set out to become as Egyptian as possible. They adopted hieroglyphic writing, started calling their leaders by the traditional titles of a pharaoh, and began to worship Egyptian gods, especially Set. Set was, of course, the chief adversary of Osiris and Horus, but Egyptians probably did not see this as an insult. Set had long held a position of honor in the Delta region. Local rulers throughout Egypt acknowledged the rule of the "Great Hyksos" and paid him tribute. It shows something about attitudes toward the legitimacy of these rulers that later king lists such as the Turin Papyrus included the names of the six pharaohs of the Hyksos 15th dynasty.

The last of these six was named Apopi. According to a story written many years later, at one point he sent a message to the prince of Thebes, Seqenenre II, complaining that he couldn't sleep in his palace at Avaris because the captive hippos in Thebes (300 miles upriver from Avaris) were making too much noise. He insisted that Seqenenre do something about it, right away.

This ridiculous demand was apparently the Hyksos equivalent of making an insulting remark about Seqenenre's mother. Seqenenre's response was to start a revolt against Hyksos rule. As his mummy shows, the revolt ended very badly for him. First he suffered an ax blow to the forehead that left him with a paralyzed arm. When, a month or two later, he managed to return to battle, he was beaten to his knees by a blow from a mace, then killed by a spear thrust behind the left ear. However, his widow, queen Ahhotep, rallied his discouraged troops. An inscription at Karnak praises her role: "She has looked after her [Egypt's] soldiers; she has guarded her . . . ; she has pacified Upper Egypt and expelled her rebels." Her coffin, found in Thebes in 1859 AD, contained a magnificent ceremonial axhead of gold and bronze, given in recognition of her courage and leadership, and three "Golden Fly" awards for valor.

After the death of Seqenenre, command of the Theban revolt passed to his older son, Kamose. Kamose later had the history of his campaign carved on two stone tablets or stelae. The first part of one is known only from a later copy, made by a schoolboy who was not very good at spelling. Fortunately, the other stela turned up half a century ago at Karnak. It had been recycled as a foundation stone for a huge statue, now gone. The two stelae tell how Kamose first won over his overly cautious advisers with a stirring speech:

> *One prince is in Avaris and another in Cush [Nubia], and here I sit associated with an Asiatic and a Nubian! Each man has his slice of this Egypt, dividing up the land with me . . . No man can settle down, when despoiled by the taxes of the Asiatics.*

His advisers were convinced. Kamose raised an army and took it northward.

After defeating a Hyksos ally near Hermopolis, halfway between Thebes and the Delta, and taking much loot, Kamose went on to lay siege to the Hyksos capital of Avaris. Apopi, who was still the Hyksos leader, hoped to convince the prince of Nubia to attack Kamose from the rear. He argued that if Kamose took Avaris, he would then turn to attack Nubia. We do not know how the Nubian prince would have responded to this appeal, because Kamose intercepted the message. He kept Apopi bottled up in his capital, but he did not have enough strength to take the walled city by assault. After a while, he and his troops went back to Thebes, leaving Avaris still in the hands of Apopi.

Not long afterward, Kamose died. He was succeeded by his younger brother, Ahmose, known to later generations as the Liberator. In a series of campaigns, Ahmose captured Avaris, then pursued the retreating Hyksos to their new base of Sharuhen, in southwestern Palestine. It took three sieges in successive years to conquer the fortified town, but at last the Hyksos menace was ended. Ahmose now turned his attention south, where the Nubian nobles were trying to hold on to their independence from Egyptian rule. One campaign followed another. Each time Ahmose thought the Nubians were pacified, another rebellion broke out. Between expeditions, though, Ahmose found time to establish the capital in his home town of Thebes, to declare that Amen was now to be regarded as "King of the Gods," and to start the enlargement of Amen's temple at Karnak. He also organized a government administration that would function, more or less unchanged, for the next 500 years.

After the death of Ahmose, around 1515 BC, his son, Amenhotep I, led his troops into Nubia and finished the job Ahmose had started. New wealth, especially gold from the Nubian mines, began to flood into Thebes. When Amenhotep died, his successor and younger brother, Thutmose I, was able to boast that his rule extended from far in the South, near the Fifth Cataract, to the marshes of the Euphrates, in Mesopotamia. This stretched the truth only slightly. The city-states of Palestine and Syria were more allies than subjects, but they did send tribute to Egypt, while carrying on a flourishing and profitable trade.

"His Majesty Herself"

Thutmose I and his queen had four children, two boys and two girls. Both boys and one of the girls died in childhood. That left only a girl, Hatshepsut. Who would occupy the Horus Throne when Thutmose I was gone? The solution to this problem was typically Egyptian. Pharaohs as a rule had other wives in addition to the Great Royal Wife, or queen. (They also kept harems of women who were concubines, not wives.) Thutmose I did have a son, also named Thutmose, by one of his secondary wives. The boy was only half royal, but that barrier was overcome by marrying him to his half sister, Hatshepsut, who was 100 percent royal. After the death of their father, Thutmose II became pharaoh and Hatshepsut became the queen.

The new royal couple had two children, both girls. Thutmose II did have a son, but the boy's mother was not even a secondary wife, but a concubine. The boy was eight or nine when Thutmose II learned from his doctors that he did not have long to live. Once again, Egypt was without an heir to the throne, a "Horus in the Nest." Once again, the solution was a dynastic marriage. The boy was wedded to his little half sister, Nefrure, and on his father's death, around 1504 BC, he took the throne as Thutmose III.

But who would rule on the boy's behalf? His mother was a harem girl, probably an ignorant peasant, maybe even a slave. Hatshepsut, still in her late twenties, was both the widow of the God Thutmose II and daughter of the Transfigured Osiris, Thutmose I, and his Great Royal Wife. By birth and training, she was fitted to command. And so she did. For the next few years, she served as regent, directing the business of government while carefully deferring to the child pharaoh and to her own small daughter, the queen.

We do not know exactly when or how this changed. We do know that, from being the power behind the throne, Hapshepsut stepped forward and took the throne itself. She had herself proclaimed Lord of the Two Lands. She posed for statues that show her with a masculine body, wearing a short kilt and royal headdress. She even donned the long, stiff artificial beard of a pharaoh. As for the boy, Thutmose III, instead of having him quietly eliminated, as many people in her situation might have done, she sent him to the temple of Amen as an apprentice priest. She even continued to give him second billing as coregent on many of her monuments.

Hatshepsut carried out this coup because she believed her birth and blood gave her a greater claim to the throne than her little son-in-law, who was barely one-quarter royal. She also distrusted the expansionist policies of her father, Thutmose I. She wanted to restore the glory of the days when Egypt had lived in splendid isolation from foreigners.

Many among the nobility and priesthood agreed with her. Her most important supporter was the high priest of Amen, a man named Hapseneb, who became her vizier. With his help, she began to spread the story that the god Amen-Re was literally her father. The god came to her mother's bedroom one night, disguised as the pharaoh. At the end of the romantic encounter, he revealed his true identity, then told the queen, "Hatshepsut shall be the name of this my daughter, whom I have placed in your body. She shall exercise the excellent kingship of this whole land."

Whether or not this propaganda influenced her people, the success of Hatshepsut's policies did. Her encouragement of trade helped enrich the country. She spent heavily on great public works projects, restoring temples and monuments that had been damaged under the Hyksos and laying the foundations of new ones. She bragged:

I have restored that which was in ruins, and I have raised up that which had been left since the foreign barbarians were in your midst, ruling in ignorance of Re. Nothing was done until the time when My Majesty was established upon the throne of Re. Then I came, flaming with indignation, and I removed this insult to the great god.

Her ally in this work was her brilliant chief architect, Senmut. He was much more than an ally to her. Among the many titles she showered on him were Hereditary Prince and Count; Sealbearer of the King of Lower Egypt; Overseer of the Fields, Gardens, Cows, Serfs, Peasant-Farmers, and Granaries of Amen; Steward of the King; Controller of Every Divine Craft; Great Father-Tutor of the Princess Nefrure; and Controller of All Construction Work of the King.

Senmut's masterpiece was the funerary temple he designed and built for Hatshepsut across the river from Thebes, at Deir el Bahri. This rivals such monuments as the Parthenon in Athens for the title of most beautiful building of the ancient world. Sited at the base of towering cliffs, it has balanced rows of colonnades on three levels, connected by long, wide ramps. Reliefs carved on the walls tell the story of Hatshepsut's miraculus conception and birth, of her coronation as pharaoh at the hands of her father, Thutmose I (an event that was pure imagination), and of the great trading mission she sent to the land of Punt.

The land of Punt was probably somewhere along what is now the coast of Somalia. When the five big Egyptian ships arrived there, the people hurried to the shore to greet them. The chief of Punt came, and so did his wife, who is shown as enormously fat, riding on a very little donkey. After some lively bartering, the Egyptians turned over their cargo of linen, pottery, bronze weapons, and jewelry, and loaded their ships with bags of fragrant myrrh gum, live myrrh trees with their roots carefully potted, ebony, ivory, panther hides, and live animals. One relief shows a ship after some baboons have escaped from their cages and scampered into the rigging. The water below the ship teems with sharks, squid, turtles, and exotic fish.

The temple at Deir el Bahri was not meant to be Hatshepsut's tomb. That was constructed in the Valley of the Kings, on the other side of the cliffs. The main corridor of the tomb is over 200 yards long and points straight toward the site of the temple. It looks as if the original idea was to tunnel completely through the cliffs and build the burial chamber directly under the temple. If so, the plan was not carried out. There is, however, an impressive tomb quarried into the bedrock under the temple, its entrance carefully concealed. This is the tomb that Senmut secretly built for himself. He also had images of himself in prayer carved in obscure corners of the sanctuary. They were so placed that they would be hidden by the open doors of storerooms and cabinets during services.

Hatshepsut occupied the Horus Throne for over 20 years. How she died is not known. Most experts think that she died a normal death. Some, however, believe that she was assassinated by Thutmose III or his partisans. Whatever the truth, once she was safely dead, Thutmose III went after her memory with a fury. Dozens of her statues were smashed and the pieces dumped in an old quarry. Her name was chiseled off monuments throughout Egypt, and especially in her temple at Deir el Bahri. Sometimes the name of Thutmose III was carved in its place, and sometimes the names of Thutmose II or even Thutmose I. In our era, this caused much confusion for some archaeologists, who took it to mean that both the earlier Thutmoses were still alive when Hatshepsut fell from power.

The mummy of Hatshepsut may have been destroyed, too;

in any case, it is one of the few royal mummies of the 18th dynasty that have not yet been definitely identified. A mummy that may be hers was found in the Valley of the Kings in 1991 AD, hidden in the tomb of the woman who had been her nurse. Whether Hatshepsut's mummy was concealed or destroyed, she got off lighter in this posthumous persecution than her close collaborator, Senmut. His hidden tomb was located and utterly wrecked. His quartzite sarcophagus—the twin of one made for Hatshepsut—was pounded into thousands of fragments and scattered across the desert. As for his mummy, we can only imagine what Thutmose III told his underlings to do to that.

The First Great General

Hatshepsut's focus on foreign trade and internal improvements may have enriched Egypt, but it also gave local rulers in the regions subdued by earlier pharaohs the hope that they could break away from Egyptian rule. When Thutmose III came to power, some 30 years had passed since the last important Egyptian military expedition. Now a league of rebels had formed in Palestine and Syria. Its leader was the prince of the city of Kadesh, on the Orontes River in northern Syria.

Word came to Thutmose that 330 Syrian princes had joined the rebellion and brought their armies to join the prince of Kadesh at the walled city of Megiddo, in Palestine. Megiddo was an important strategic fortress that commanded the crucial north-south trade route between Egypt and Syria. It is better known to Christians under the name of Armageddon, the site of the apocalyptic battle prophesied to take place at the end of the world.

Thutmose acted at once. He assembled an army of 20,000

at Tharu, on Egypt's northeast frontier, and marched them north. At the head of the army, a chariot carried the golden ram's-head standard of Amen. Thutmose followed, surrounded by the royal bodyguard. A team of black stallions pulled his gold-bedecked chariot. On his head was the *khepresh,* the battle crown of blue leather studded with gold. This was no leisurely parade, however. Thutmose pushed his troops. They reached Gaza, 160 miles from Tharu, in just ten days and pushed on northward. A week later, the Egyptian forces were in Yehem, on the southern slope of the Carmel Mountains. On the north side, across the ridge, was the plain of Megiddo.

What happened then (or at least the official version), we know from a long inscription carved into the wall of the temple of Karnak. There were three routes to Megiddo. Two were roundabout; the third was much shorter, but led through the narrow pass of Aruna, where the army would have to go in single file, an easy target for ambush. At a council of war, Thutmose's officers advised him to take one of the longer but safer routes. Of course, as a god, he rejected this prudence:

> *As I live, as Re loves me, as my father Amen favors me, and as I am rejuvenated with life and power, My Majesty will proceed along this Aruna road. Let him of you who wishes go upon those [other] roads you speak of, and let him of you who wishes come in the train of My Majesty . . .*

Of course, all his advisers agreed to follow him. Some of them must have privately expected a disaster, but they went along.

It took a whole day for the Egyptian army, with Thutmose and his gilded chariot in the lead, to file through the narrow pass and make the descent to the plain of Megiddo. During that whole day, the Syrians watched passively, when they could so easily have destroyed their opponents piecemeal. Perhaps they still expected the main Egyptian force to take one of the easier routes. By nightfall Thutmose had most of his army over the treacherous pass and camped on the plain. The Syrian princes and their soldiers camped between them and the city walls.

At daybreak the two armies lined up facing each other. Thutmose, arrayed like Horus, mounted his chariot, raised his arm, and led the charge. For a moment the Syrians watched as if paralyzed. Then, without shooting an arrow or raising a lance, they turned and ran for the safety of the walled town. Those who got there first slammed and barred the gates against the foe. The tardy were trapped between the walls and the approaching Egyptians. Frantically they called for help. The townspeople who were nervously watching the battle from atop the wall stripped off their clothes to make cloth ropes and began to haul them up the sides of the walls.

The Egyptians might easily have taken the town and won the war, but they didn't. Overcome by the sight of all the horses, chariots, weapons, tents, and miscellaneous baggage that the Syrians had left on the field, the troops of Thutmose fell to looting. True, they later presented their trophies to their pharaoh, but that was not much consolation. "Had you captured this city," Thutmose told them, "I would have given many sacrifices to Re this day; because every prince of every country that has revolted is within it; and because the capture of Megiddo is the capture of a thousand towns!"

The only recourse now was a siege. The Egyptians surrounded the town and settled down to wait. It was soon harvesttime, and the hungry people of Megiddo had to watch from their walls as the besiegers gathered in their crops. After several months, they had no choice but to give up. The prince of Kadesh, the leader of the rebellion, escaped to his own city. The other Syrian princelings sent their children through the gate carrying their armor and weapons to lay at the feet of Thutmose, while they "stood on their walls, giving praise to My Majesty, seeking that the breath of life might be given to them."

Surprisingly, Thutmose agreed. After they swore an oath of loyalty to him, he let them go home . . . but on donkeyback. Their 2,000 horses were prizes of war, along with over 900 chariots, vast herds of cattle, flocks of sheep, and countless swords, lances, and daggers. Thutmose also took back to Egypt 87 children of the Syrian princes as hostages for their fathers' good behavior. In later years, many of these little princes and princesses would return to govern their home cities with an Egyptian education and Egyptian sympathies.

On his return to Thebes, Thutmose paraded his army and the captured loot through the streets, before amazed and enthusiastic crowds. Then, in a grand ceremony in the temple at Karnak, he gave most of the booty to the priests of Amen. He also turned over to the king of the gods, whom he credited with his victory, the yearly tribute from three towns in Syria, extensive farms in Lower and Upper Egypt, and herds of captured Syrian cattle to stock the farms. This presentation of regal gifts to Amen was to become a fixed custom of the 18th dynasty.

Another fixed custom during the next 20 years was the annual military expedition. Each spring after the first harvest, Thutmose and his army set off, usually northward. Most of these efforts were more like excursions than campaigns. Not many people wanted to test the fighting strength of the pharaoh. Soon Thutmose had brought all of Palestine and Lebanon, and most of Syria, under his rule. Not that Egyptian rule was very strict. As long as a city-state paid its yearly tribute on time and did not do anything to encourage the enemies of Egypt, Thutmose was content to let its ruler manage local affairs as he saw fit.

One expedition later in his reign was much more strenuous even than the siege of Megiddo. Stretching across the upper Euphrates Valley, and well beyond, was a rival power, the Mitanni Empire. Not much is known today about this culture, except that they were horsemen who may have come from the area that is now northern India. Archaeologists have still not found the Mitanni capital, Wassukanni. Thutmose's quarrel with the Mitanni was that they backed the prince of Kadesh in his rebellion, which continued off and on after the Egyptian victory at Megiddo.

In preparation for the campaign, Thutmose had many ships built of Lebanese cedar at Byblos, on the Mediterranean coast. These "were placed on carts, with oxen pulling them, and they journeyed in front of My Majesty, in order to cross the great river." The records do not say how many weeks it took the poor, overburdened oxen to drag the boats across 250 miles of rugged countryside to the Euphrates. Along the way, the Egyptians conquered several important cities. When they reached the lands of the Mitanni, the king fled downriver. Thutmose followed in his cedar boats and ravaged the land. Before taking the road homeward, he set up a victory stela on the riverbank, next to the one that had been erected by his grandfather, Thutmose I.

By now Thutmose was, for his time, middle-aged, but showed no sign of slowing down. When he was not off touring his new empire at the head of his army, he traveled up and down the Nile Valley, inspecting all the temples, irrigation canals, and other projects he was building or restoring. At Heliopolis the entrance pylon of his new temple was flanked by two enormous obelisks. One of these is now on the Thames Embankment in London, and the other in New York's Central Park.

Egypt was now the richest and most powerful nation in the world. The country's location, at the crossroads of Africa, Asia, and the Mediterranean basin, contributed to this, of course, as did its natural resources. Wealth also came flooding in from its possessions in Palestine and Syria to the northeast and Nubia to the south. Most important, however, were the country's advanced culture and technology. People in Greece, Asia Minor, and Mesopotamia wanted Egyptian pottery, cloth, and metal goods because they were known as the best. The physicians, architects, engineers, and scribes of Egypt were called the world's finest. Under Thutmose, the Egyptian army was also also among the best. One of the world's oldest civilizations was also, in the 18th dynasty, one of its most successful.

The pharaohs of the 18th dynasty were the first rulers of Egypt who were natives of Thebes. They saw their rise to wealth and power as a sign of the favor of Amen, the god most worshiped at Thebes. They passed on much of their wealth, and the power that went with it, to the temples and priests of Amen. Other gods had a much longer history—Re, Ptah, Thoth, Anubis, and of course, the divine family of Osiris, Isis, and their son, Horus. These other gods had their important temples and cult centers, too. But none had anything to compare with the stupefyingly huge temple of Amen at Karnak, and none had the riches to support the equally huge corps of priests and temple workers.

Above all, no other god had come to be called "king of the gods." Each new victory, each new trade expedition, brought a larger proportion of the booty to Amen. The priests who controlled this wealth began to pass their offices on from father to son. They used their power to demand ever greater tribute and privileges. As long as the empire was expanding, as long as new riches were flowing into Egypt and its splendid capital at Thebes, these demands could be met without obvious harm, and so they were. But that would change.

Soon the shadow of Karnak began to loom over the whole country. Fifty years after the death of Thutmose III, the temple of Amen was said to own as much as one third of all the fertile land in Egypt, with huge herds and flocks and hordes of slaves. It owned many farms, orchards, and even whole towns in the Asian territories as well. Every year hundreds of pounds of gold from the mines of Nubia and the Eastern Desert were turned over to the temple. Its storehouses and granaries rivaled those of the pharaohs. So did its power.

The two parties, of Pharaoh, the god-king, and of Amen, the king of the gods, were on a collision course. The crash, when it came, was to lead to one of the most mysterious and controversial periods in the entire 3,000-year history of Egypt.

"That Criminal of Akhetaten"

Two hundred fifty miles down the Nile from Thebes, almost halfway to Memphis, the cliffs that form the eastern rim of the valley draw in next to the river. For some 20 miles there is nothing on that side but sheer walls of rock, dotted with birds' nests. Then the cliffs recede, to make a half circle around a section of bleak desert eight miles long and four miles wide.

Today the site is known as el Amarna, after one of the tiny villages that cling to the narrow strip of cultivation next to the river. For one brief period, though, a splendid city flourished on this unpromising ground. This was Akhetaten, "the Horizon of the Aten" and the capital of Egypt. Then, as hastily as it had been built, it was deserted and razed to the ground. The site was abandoned to the prowling jackals and drifting sand.

As for the pharaoh who built the city, his name was left off the lists of kings. His temples and monuments were smashed and the rubble used as fill. Later historians knew nothing of him or the reasons he inspired such loathing and fear in those who came after him. His memory had been blotted out, seemingly forever.

Beginning in the 1820s, a few Europeans went to el Amarna. They were drawn by rumors of strange decorations in the tombs cut into the cliffs. And strange, they were. Instead of the usual heroic kings and animal-headed gods, there were carvings of a royal couple depicted with a realism that was almost cartoonlike. Instead of the usual solemn state occasions, they were shown feasting, riding in chariots, and playing affectionately with their tiny children. There were murals of religious ceremonies—but where was the image of the god? In its place was a peculiar disk from which radiating lines came down, each ending in a hand. Clearly there was some mystery attached to this place.

In 1887 a woman from one of the nearby villages went into the desert and began to dig. She was looking for *sebakh,* the nitrogen-rich fertilizer that forms from decayed mud bricks. Instead of *sebakh,* her shovel uncovered dozens of rectangular pieces of baked clay. She must have been irritated at first. But when she saw that the clay pieces were covered with lines of wedge-shaped marks, she dug deeper. She had no idea what the objects were. She simply hoped they might be worth something. Like every Egyptian peasant, she had heard the rumors that almost any piece of old junk could turn out to be valuable. By the end of the day, she had collected over 300 of the little clay tablets. She sold them to a neighbor, who sold them to a dealer, and so on. At last they fell into the hands of someone who recognized the marks for what they were: cuneiform, the writing of ancient Babylon.

Never before had any Babylonian tablets been found in Egypt. That fact made some scholars sure that these had to be fakes. Others thought they might be genuine. One of these was E. A. Wallis Budge, a cuneiform expert who was able to translate the tablets. Most of them turned out to be official messages from cities in Syria and Palestine, written in Akkadian, the international language of diplomacy in the

14th century BC. They were addressed to a pharaoh whose name few Egyptologists had even heard of: Akhenaten.

Within months after this find become known, the great British archaeologist W. M. Flinders Petrie began digging at el Amarna. Under the drifted sand he found the remains of great palaces and temples as well as the villas of nobles and the houses and workshops of more humble folk. All was in ruins, but Petrie found tiles and plaster floors painted with flowers, plants, and birds in a style so fluid that it seemed positively un-Egyptian. In what had been the city's garbage dump, he painstakingly collected the fragments of clay seals from ancient wine and oil jugs. The markings on these told him that the mysterious Akhenaten had ruled Egypt for 17 years. But who was he, and why had he been cut out of history?

The story emerged only gradually. Many important details have been lost, probably forever. Akhenaten was a younger son of the pharaoh Amenhotep III and his wife, queen Tiy, and was originally given his father's name, which means "Amen is satisfied." Amenhotep III ruled at the very height of Egypt's wealthiest period. He lived in such style that archaeologists call him Amenhotep the Magnificent. His new temples and palaces dominated the landscape up and down the Nile. The palace he built for his queen, across from Thebes, included a mile-long artificial lake for boating parties. The two gigantic statues famous in later times as the Colossi of Memnon were merely the gatekeepers for his now-vanished mortuary temple.

Like his predecessors in the 18th dynasty, Amenhotep gave lavish gifts to the cult of Amen. However, during his reign the name of another god, the Aten, began to gain prominence. This name was not new. For centuries it had been used to refer to the visible, physical disk of the sun. The sun god, Re-Herakhte, was often shown carrying it atop his falcon head. Now it came to be the name of a separate divinity, "Re of the Disk, supreme power whose forms are his transformations when he makes his appearance as the Aten." Amenhotep even named his royal state barge "The Radiance of the Aten."

The future Akhenaten became his father's heir when his older brother, Thutmose, died. Egyptologists are still arguing fiercely over whether he ruled jointly with his father for some time, and if so, for how long. In any case, soon after he took the throne, he began to show that his attachment to the worship of the Aten was more than casual. He ordered the building of new temples in Thebes dedicated to the Aten. Unlike the dark, gloomy, overpowering temples of Amen, these were open to the sky and the sunlight. His wife, Nefertiti, who may also have been his cousin or half sister, was just as devoted as he. She took part in rituals at her husband's side and established her own temple, the Mansion of the Benben, which housed the choir singers of the temple of the Aten.

In the fifth year of his reign, around 1345 BC, the young pharaoh Amenhotep IV gathered his courtiers and high officials for an astonishing announcement. His divine father, the Aten, had granted him an inspiration. He was to seek out the place where the world had first come into being and to build there a city devoted to the worship of the Aten. From now on, he would be known as Akhenaten, "It is well with the Aten." He went on to explain that the Aten was not like other gods, who were only images created and tended by priests. The Aten was the only god, universal, eternal, and all-powerful, who created himself anew each morning, as he had since before the beginning of the world.

> *Thy rising is fair in the horizon of heaven, O living Aten, Beginner of Life. When thou dawnest in the East, thou fillest every land with thy beauty. Thou art indeed beautiful, great, radiant, and high over every land . . . Thou art remote yet thy rays are upon the earth. Thou art in the sight of men, yet thy ways are not known . . .*
>
> *Thou drivest away the night when thou givest forth thy beams. The Two Lands are in festival. They awake and stand upon their feet, for thou hast raised them up . . . All cattle are at peace in their pastures. The trees and meadows grow green. The birds fly from their nests, raising their wings in praise of thy spirit. All the sheep dance on their feet, all winged things fly, they live when thou hast risen for them . . . The fish in the river leap in thy presence. Thy rays are in the midst of the sea . . .*
>
> *Thou makest the waters under the earth and thou bringest them forth [as the Nile] at thy pleasure, to sustain the people of Egypt, even as thou hast made them live for thee, O Divine Lord of them all, toiling for them, the Lord of every land, shining forth for them, the Aten of the day time, great in majesty!*

This great hymn to the Aten was most likely written by Akhenaten himself. It sounds amazingly similar to some of the Psalms in the Hebrew Bible. Sigmund Freud was so impressed with these similarities that he suggested Moses learned his monotheism and his hatred of graven images from contact with the religion of the Aten. Although there is no real evidence for this idea, it is striking to read the words of an Egyptian pharaoh of the 14th century BC and then hear them echoed in a work as familiar to our time as the Bible.

Akhenaten was not content to proclaim his devotion to the Aten and build a new capital in the god's honor. He ordered the temples of the old gods shut down. Their lands and treasures were returned to the state and their priests were dispersed. The Theban god, Amen, so recently hailed as the "king of the gods," was the biggest target of this campaign. Masons working for the crown fanned out to chisel his name off the walls of temples, tombs, statues, and stelae. They even defaced (very carefully) the hieroglyphs for Amen in the name of Akhenaten's own father, Amenhotep.

Along with the new religion came a new approach to art. The rules for painting and sculpting had been the same since before the time of the pyramids, 1,500 years earlier. The head of a person was always in profile, the torso facing the viewer, and the legs in profile. A king, like a god, was always tall, slim, and broad-shouldered. If a row of lotus blossoms was shown, each was exactly like its neighbors. The same was true for a row of soldiers or servants.

Akhenaten changed this. He proclaimed that art should obey the demands of *ma'at,* a word that can be translated as "truth" or "sincerity." At first the results were rather peculiar. Early statues of Akhenaten, found in the ruins of the temple of the Aten at Thebes, show him with an elongated head, enormous ears, narrow, sloping shoulders, wide, almost feminine hips, and a potbelly. When compared to all the idealized statues of earlier pharaohs, these looked very odd, even deformed. Some Egyptologists decided Akhenaten must have suffered from a serious glandular condition called Frohlich's syndrome. This idea ran into trouble when others pointed out that the victims of Frohlich's are sterile. We know that Akhenaten and Nefertiti had six daughters, and there is reason to think he may have had other children by secondary wives.

The principle of *ma'at* applied to the subjects of art as well as the technique. In place of stylized battle scenes, the king is shown at home with his family. One limestone carving shows Akhenaten and Nefertiti sitting facing each other. Akhenaten is lifting one of their small daughters to give her a kiss. Nefertiti is holding two others. The one on her knee is pointing to her father and clearly making an amused comment. The other is standing on Nefertiti's lap and reaching up to play with one of her earrings. At the top of the scene is the Aten. Its rays reach down to hold ankhs, the symbol of life, next to the nostrils of the king and queen.

In 1912 a group of German archaeologists led by Ludwig Borchardt were excavating at el Amarna. The site where they were digging turned out to be the home and workshop of Akhenaten's chief sculptor, Thutmose. Part of his work was creating stone heads of the royal family, to be used as models by other sculptors throughout the kingdom. When the city of Akhetaten was abandoned, some of these models were left behind, to be found in our era by the German team. One of them was a painted limestone bust of Nefertiti. Now in the Berlin Museum, it is known worldwide as a symbol of ideal beauty. Yet once, this object, one of the greatest relics of ancient Egypt, was thrown away as worthless. Its serene yet vibrant personality shows us the direction the artistic innovation of the Amarna period was taking and hints at the heights of achievement it may have reached in its last years.

In the 12th year of Akhenaten's reign, a great jubilee was held in the splendid new temple of the Aten in the splendid new city of the Aten. While ambassadors from all points of the compass waited in the open courtyard, Akhenaten and Nefertiti were carried in on palanquins or litters of gold. Surrounded by their family and court, they accepted the exotic treasures sent as gifts by the kings of other countries. Not all the other rulers were pleased by what they heard about this ceremony. The king of Assyria later wrote angrily to Akhenaten, "Why are my messengers kept standing in the open sun? They will die in the open sun. If it does the pharaoh good to stand in the open sun, then let the pharaoh stand there and die in the open sun!"

Some foreign rulers sensed an opportunity in the situation. If the king of Egypt was preoccupied by his new religion, maybe he would not notice if his outlying possessions were snatched away. There were rich cities in Syria and Lebanon that had been subject to Egypt for half a century or more, since the days of Thutmose III. Now they found themselves attacked by neighbors who were secretly backed by the Hittite Empire in Asia Minor. Worse, these neighbors had influential agents at the court of Akhenaten who seem to have kept him from grasping the situation. Before long, even nearby Palestine was under attack. For whatever reason, Akhenaten did not react.

One reason may have been the situation at home. Akhenaten and Nefertiti obviously adored their six daughters. But a daughter, however much adored, was not a son, and that was what was needed for the succession. Desperate, Akhenaten wedded his eldest daughter, Meritaten, to a boy named Smenkhkare, and made Smenkhkare his coruler. Practically nothing is known of Smenkhkare, except that he established a temple in Thebes, dedicated to Amen. Clearly the grip of Akhenaten's religious reform was starting to slip.

Records of Akhenaten's last years are sparse and confusing. His second daughter apparently died in childbirth; a touching tomb painting shows Akhenaten and his family pouring sand over their heads in mourning. His third daughter, Ankhesenpaaten, was married while still a child to a boy even younger than she. His name was Tutankhaten, and he may have been a son of Akhenaten by a lesser wife.

Akhenaten died in the 17th year of his reign. Deprived of its founder and guide, his new religion and new city began to die too. Nobles and courtiers closed up their villas and returned to Thebes. Merchants, craftsmen, and artists followed. When Tutankhaten became king at the age of nine, he changed his name to Tutankh*amen* and moved the capital back to Thebes. Once there, he began to restore to the cult of Amen all the wealth and power Akhenaten had tried to take away.

Tutankhamen and his queen, now called Ankhesenamen, were still too young to exert real power. They had to depend on the vizier, a middle-aged man named Ay, and the head of the armies, General Horemheb. Both men had held high office under Akhenaten. Both were now closely allied to the priesthood of Amen. When, still in his teens, Tutankhamen died, Ay seized power. He may also have tried to force a marriage on Ankhesenamen, to make his claim to rule more legitimate.

Frantic, the young widow wrote secretly to the Hittite king. Would he send her a prince she could marry and put on the throne of Egypt? The Hittite king, suspicious, stalled. Finally he did send one of his sons. By this time the scheme had been discovered. The Hittite prince was ambushed and killed by Egyptian soldiers in Palestine. Ankhesenamen's name stopped appearing in the records soon afterward.

Inscriptions from Ay's brief reign did not even mention Akhenaten, Smenkhkare, and Tutankhamen. He clearly wanted to give an impression that he had come to the throne right after Amenhotep III. It was his successor, Horemheb, however, who tried to wipe out the memory of the entire Amarna period and its worship of the Aten. The temples Akhenaten had built at Karnak and Akhetaten were razed to the ground. With the rubble, Horemheb built new temples dedicated to the glory of Amen and the pharaoh Horemheb. Akhenaten was never referred to by name, only as "that criminal of Akhetaten."

The 18th dynasty began with Ahmose the Liberator and took Egypt to the heights of power, wealth, and culture. It came to an end with what amounted to a military coup. History has its ironies, though. Only experts recall the name and deeds of Horemheb. But what of the queen whose memory he tried to erase? Over 3,000 years later, the face of Nefertiti is known and admired throughout the world. And the child pharaoh he dominated? Even people who know nothing else about ancient Egypt recognize the name of Tutankhamen . . . "King Tut."

THE LONG, SLOW EBB

The young man who became pharaoh around 1280 BC was tall, slim, and athletic. The blood of warriors ran in his veins. His grandfather, Ramses I, had been the head of Horemheb's armies before rising to the throne. His father, Seti I, had begun the difficult and delicate process of reconquering Egypt's vassal territories in Palestine and Syria. Now, as Ramses II, the new pharaoh vowed to finish the job.

The most important obstacle to his project was the Hittite Empire. The Hittite king, Muwatallis, was the grandson of the king who had missed the chance to wed one of his sons to the widow of Tutankhamen and perhaps gain the Egyptian throne for his family. Muwatallis did not have such grandiose ambitions, but he saw Syria as an important part of the Hittite sphere of influence. No 22-year-old pharaoh was going to take it away from him. He began to assemble an army.

When couriers brought Ramses word that the Hittites were marching toward the Syrian city of Kadesh, he saw his opportunity to win a great victory. He quickly led his army onto the route north. Its 20,000 soldiers and charioteers were organized into four divisions that marched under the banners of four powerful gods of Egypt, Amen, Re, Ptah, and Sutekh. Many of those who marched were not themselves Egyptian, though. They were mercenaries or draftees from subject territories in Libya, Nubia, and Palestine.

Twenty-nine days after crossing the Egyptian border, Ramses and his army reached the heights overlooking the plain of Kadesh. The walled city ten miles to the north was well protected on three sides by the Orontes River, but nowhere was there any sign of Hittite soldiers. Nor had Ramses' scouts come across any trace of the enemy. Confident of an easy victory, Ramses ordered his army to camp for the night on the heights. Early the next morning, he led his personal bodyguard and the Amen division down toward the undefended city. The other three divisions were to follow.

Ramses was getting ready to ford the Orontes when his scouts brought him two captured Hittite deserters. They had good news to tell him. Muwatallis had been at Kadesh earlier, but when he learned that mighty Pharaoh was coming, he became terrified and fled north to the distant city of Aleppo. This was what Ramses wanted to hear. He pushed ahead with his bodyguard. The Amen division trailed after him. The Re division was a couple of miles behind them, and the rest of his army was still up in the hills.

Just west of Kadesh, Ramses set up camp and called his officers to a council of war. By now the Amen division had managed to catch up to him. In the middle of the session, two more captured locals were brought in. They told a very different story from the two "deserters." The Hittites had not retreated in fear to Aleppo. In fact, their army was concealed on the opposite side of Kadesh, preparing to ambush the Egyptians.

Before Ramses could react to this shock, the Hittite chariots attacked the unsuspecting Re division, a couple of miles down the valley. The Egyptians broke in panic and ran, half back toward the hills and the other half toward Ramses' camp. Not just toward the camp, but through it, carrying with them most of the dazed and terrified Amen division.

Ramses was left all alone, surrounded by 2,500 Hittite chariots, each carrying three men. At least, that was the official version. "My infantry and chariotry melted away before them, not one stood firm to fight." So Ramses, outnumbered several thousand to one, did what any self-respecting god-king would do. He jumped into his chariot, called on his divine father Amen for strength, and charged. Six times he attacked the circling chariots. The Hittites "became heaps of corpses before my horses."

It makes a great story, and Ramses did his best to spread it afterward. One thing is clear: Even if some of his officers and bodyguards stayed by his side, he was caught in a terrible trap. He was certainly in great danger of being captured or killed. What saved him was that most of the Hittites were more tempted by the rich booty in the deserted Egyptian camp than by the battle itself. While they were busy looting, a party of Egyptian allies from the coast came on the scene unexpectedly and attacked them from the rear. They were later joined by soldiers of the Amen and Re divisions who had recovered from their panic enough to come back.

Near nightfall, the Ptah division arrived to turn the tide. The Hittites withdrew to the safety of the walled city, while Ramses hurriedly took what was left of his army back to Egypt. Once there, he proclaimed a mighty victory. Sculptors carved huge reliefs of Ramses smiting the Asiatics on temple walls at Karnak, Luxor, Abydos, Abu Simbel . . . all over Egypt. A hundred years ago, archaeologists were so impressed by the records of this exploit that they started calling him Ramses the Great. Then the facts about the battle of Kadesh became clear. As a general, Ramses was a blockhead who fell for an obvious trick. He survived only by a combination of blind courage and dumb luck.

Archaeologists were also impressed by the countless monuments that bore the name of Ramses II. With reason—some of the most imposing buildings in Egypt were put up during his reign. These include the Hypostyle Hall at Karnak, the Ramesseum in western Thebes, and the temple at Abu Simbel, with its four 70-foot-high statues of Ramses guarding the front. He also built a new capital city at Tanis, in the Delta, and renamed it Pi-Ramses. Its palaces, temples, canals, and bustling port made it the greatest city of its time. One of its most imposing features was a colossal 90-foot-tall statue of Ramses. Thebes, the former capital far upriver, became a sleepy religious center.

Building all these monumental structures was not enough glory for Ramses. He also had a habit of carving his own name on temples, monuments, obelisks, and stelae put up by earlier pharaohs. One observer suggested that if he could have lined the entire Nile with statues of himself, he would have done it gladly.

In at least two spheres, Ramses definitely deserved to be called great. First, he lived a very long time, about 85 years, 67 of which he spent on the throne. Second, during those years he fathered at least 100 sons and 50 daughters, with help from seven successive Great Royal Wives and an army of lesser wives and legal concubines. One after another, a dozen crown princes grew old and died waiting for their father to finish his journey from the throne to the tomb.

For 20 years after the battle of Kadesh, Egyptian and Hittite armies pushed each other around Syria and Palestine, capturing, losing, and recapturing towns. At last, weary of the bloody stalemate, the two powers signed a peace treaty. This was the first recorded international treaty in history. Amazingly, both sides honored it. In fact, some 50 years later, Ramses' successor lived up to a mutual-aid clause in the treaty by sending grain to the Hittites during a famine.

To seal the new friendly relations between Egypt and the Hittites, the Hittite king sent his daughter to wed Ramses. Naturally, she was accompanied by a throng of courtiers and soldiers and by a regal dowry. The members of her escort got along very well with the Egyptian soldiers. "They ate and drank together, being of one heart like brothers, for peace and brotherhood were between them." Since many of the soldiers on both sides were from the same areas in Syria and Palestine, it is possible that some of them really were brothers, or at least cousins. As for the pharaoh, when he met his newest bride, he "saw that she was fair of face like a goddess . . . She was beautiful in the heart of His Majesty, and he loved her more than anything."

Invasion of the Sea People

Ramses II died around 1212 BC. He was succeeded by his thirteenth son, Merneptah, who was already in middle age. Merneptah shared his father's taste for colossal stonework. He would have liked to spend his reign carving his name on other people's monuments and putting up his own. In his fifth year on the throne, however, Egypt faced its first serious threat of invasion since the days of the Hyksos, 400 years earlier. This time the danger came from the west, from the coastal region of Libya.

Egyptians called the new invaders "Sea People." We know them by other names: Achaeans, Lycians, Sardinians, and Sicilians. Something—famine, disease, pressure from other peoples still farther away—had set whole populations in motion. Driving their herds, carrying their belongings, they moved relentlessly from the vast regions north of the Black Sea down into Asia Minor. Some continued south, into Syria. Others crossed the Balkans into the Greek and Italian peninsulas. Egypt was not the only country under assault. The Hittite Empire was tottering, and so were the legendary civilizations along the Tigris and Euphrates.

Merneptah was no warrior king. After he asked a blessing from his namesake, Ptah, the god came to him in a dream and gave him a sword. Encouraged by this, Merneptah sent his armies off to the Libyan border to repel the invaders. They did. Afterward Merneptah put up a victory stela, carved on the back of a stela that had belonged to Amenhotep III. According to the inscription, more than 6,000 of the enemy were killed and 9,000 captured. These numbers give us some idea of how big the invasion must have been.

Merneptah's stela is famous among Egyptologists because of one particular line in a long, bombastic poem about the military campaign:

> *Israel is laid waste, his seed is not*

This is the only reference to Israel that has ever been found in an inscription from ancient Egypt. Egypt, of course, is often mentioned in the Bible, but for the Egyptians, the people of Israel and Judah were simply one of many peoples they grouped together as "Asiatics."

The reference on Merneptah's stela is not evidence that there were Hebrews among the invaders. In his list of those who had been pacified by Merneptah's glorious army, the scribe apparently dragged in the names of every foreign people he had ever heard of. Among these were some that other records of the time show were definitely at peace with Egypt at the time.

Merneptah's stela does have an important bearing on the subject of the historical bases for biblical accounts, however. It tells us that, by the time of his reign, the people of Israel were already known as a specific, defined group living in Palestine. The implication is that whatever the historical source for the biblical account of the Exodus, it must have taken place sometime earlier than Merneptah's reign. Since the Bible also recounts that the captive Israelites worked on building the cities of Pithom and Ramses, which were constructed largely by Merneptah's father, Ramses II, it seems to follow that the Exodus must have taken place during the reign of Ramses II. Unfortunately, there is not a single reference to such an event in any of the Egyptian inscriptions and documents that have survived.

Merneptah had won his battle, but the Sea People did not go away. Forty years later another pharaoh, who took the name of Ramses III, was at war with them again. This time the battlefields were inside the borders of Egypt, in the Nile Delta, and there were new tribes added to the invaders. These included the Danaoi, fresh from the siege of Troy, and the Philistines, who took possession of the coastal plain of Palestine. Most troubling, the Philistines were armed with a new kind of sword that sliced through the bronze weapons and armor of the Egyptians. The Iron Age had come to Egypt.

Ramses III managed to keep the Sea People from taking over the Delta, but the old empire in Palestine and Syria was gone for good. Egypt was finished as a world power. It was once more what it had been centuries earlier, the Land of the Nile.

During the reign of Ramses III, the capital at Tanis was as rich and splendid as ever. However, the countryside was in bad shape and getting worse. As the income from agriculture and trade dropped, the priesthood of Amen at Karnak demanded an even greater share of the country's wealth to make up for their shortfalls. By now the temple owned 750,000 acres of arable land (about an eighth of all the arable land in the country), over 400 orchards, 420,000 head of livestock, 65 villages, 83 ships, and 46 workshops, along with a workforce of over 80,000, most of them slaves. All of these possessions, along with the income from them, were traditionally exempt from taxes.

At the same time that the priests were tightening their grip on the economy, they were also adding new religious holidays to the calendar. Naturally this was popular with ordinary people, at least at first. Who could object to an extra day off work, with a colorful parade and free bread and beer for all? By the time of Ramses III, the *Opet* festival at Thebes lasted a full 27 days, and that was only one of a host of holidays.

The government bureaucracy began to stagger under this load. Around 1165 BC came the first recorded strike in history. The workers at Deir el Medina, who for generations had excavated, carved, and decorated the royal tombs in the Valley of the Kings, were not paid their salary in grain for two months in a row. After their pleas and protests had no effect, they walked off the job and held a sit-in at the Ramesseum, the mortuary temple of Ramses II. They told their superiors:

> *We have come to this place because of hunger and thirst. We have no clothing, no oil, no fish, no vegetables. Write to Pharaoh, our good lord, about it . . . Act so that we may live!*

The officials hurriedly gave them one month's back rations, and they went back to work. Even so, over the next few months they had to stage several more walkouts before their grievances were finally settled.

Along with history's first strike, the reign of Ramses III also gave us history's first murder mystery. It had all the right ingredients for a best-seller: sorcery, riches, royalty, infidelity, intrigue in high society, and a plot to seize the throne of the god-king himself.

The chief plotter was one of Ramses' queens, Ti. Her plan was to make her own son, Prince Pentewere, the heir to Ramses in place of the acknowledged crown prince. Some of the harem officials were in on it with her. Using witchcraft as well as poison, they tried to murder the pharaoh. It is not quite clear whether they succeeded. The commission set up to investigate the plot had its charter from Ramses III. However, in the documents of the trial, the expression used to refer to him indicates that he is dead. Maybe he survived the effects of the plot just long enough to arrest the plotters and order them brought to trial.

The trial had its odd moments. While it was going on, two of the judges went out partying with some of the defendants. The rest of the judges did not take this lightly:

> *Sentence was carried out by cutting off their noses and ears, because they had disregarded the instructions they had been given.*

More then 40 plotters were tried. Once convicted, the majority were promptly executed. Those of higher rank—including the pretender prince, who was naturally of royal blood—received different treatment. They were spared the shame of being executed and given a chance to do the honorable thing:

> *They found them guilty and left them in their own hands in the Place of Examination. They took their own lives; no penalty was carried out against them.*

After the death of Ramses III, eight more pharaohs named Ramses sat on the Horus Throne. None of them did anything of much note. Under Ramses VI, Egypt stopped working the mines in the Sinai that had been the source of so much wealth. Under Ramses IX, the tomb robbers in Thebes became so bold that they were able to buy accomplices in high office. Under Ramses XI, the high priest of Amen had a scene carved on the temple wall in which his figure was as tall as the figure of the pharaoh. Political reality had overcome the strict conventions of Egyptian art.

It was also during the reign of Ramses XI that a general named Herihor became viceroy of Nubia and commander in chief of the army. Not long afterward, he added the titles of vizier of Upper Egypt, then high priest of Amen. Now his prestige was greater than that of anyone except the pharaoh himself. As for real power, even the pharaoh could not equal him. Around 1080 BC, Herihor took the next logical step and donned the crown. He named his son the new high priest and army commander.

Egypt had started its rise with the unification of the Two Kingdoms under Menes. In those early days, political and religious authority was concentrated in the person of the god-king. Now, 2,000 years later, another pharaoh had joined church and state under his rule. There was an important difference, though. Herihor wore the crown of a pharaoh, but he did not rule both the Two Kingdoms. His power extended only over Upper Egypt. At Tanis, in the Delta, a new dynasty of merchant princes took control. The unity of the country had been fractured. Never again would it be healed for long.

In 1891 AD some peasants in the village of El Hibeh, in Upper Egypt, came across a much-damaged papyrus roll. They sold it to a dealer, who promptly resold it to a Russian Egyptologist who carried it back to Saint Petersburg. It turned out to be a report written during the time of Herihor by a temple official named Wenamen. The priests of Amen had decided to build a splendid new ceremonial barge to carry the god during festivals. They ordered Wenamen to go to Lebanon to buy fine cedar logs for the barge. He was furnished with official letters of introduction, the equivalent of several thousand dollars in gold and silver, and a small but very holy image known as Amen of the Road.

From the start, Wenamen's mission was a prime illustration of the adage that anything that can go wrong, will. At Tanis he gave his letters of introduction to the ruler, who put him aboard a Syrian cargo vessel that was leaving immediately for Lebanon. Once at sea, Wenamen realized that his letters of introduction were still back in Tanis, but the skipper of the boat refused to turn back for them.

After several days at sea, the boat arrived at Dor, a small port in Palestine. The local king, Bedel, politely sent a gift of bread and wine to the envoy of Amen-Re. Too much wine, perhaps; when Wenamen woke up, he discovered that one of the sailors had slipped into his cabin and made off with the gold and silver. He rushed to the palace and announced that since the theft had occurred in Bedel's harbor, the king had to make good his loss. Instead of throwing him out, Bedel replied, "If the thief belonged to my land . . . I would advance you the sum from my treasury while they were finding the culprit. But the thief who robbed you belonged to your ship. Tarry, however, a few days with me and I will seek him."

When the search turned up nothing, Wenamen continued his voyage. Along the way he paused to seize the money of a group of merchants who had the bad luck to be related to the people of Dor. In his report he explains this act of piracy as a simple matter of compensation. At Byblos, the prince, Zakar-Baal, would not even see him. Wenamen camped aboard his ship and waited. Every day for a month, Zakar-Baal sent one of his officials with a simple message, "Get out of my harbor!" Then a miracle happened (perhaps with a little help from some of the stolen silver). During a temple ceremony, one of Zakar-Baal's pages had a prophetic seizure and cried out, "Bring up the God! Bring up the messenger who is carrying him! It is Amen who sent him here!"

Zakar-Baal did not dare disregard this public command from heaven. He sent for Wenamen and asked what he wanted. Wenamen had not picked up any new diplomatic skills on his journey. He told the prince that Byblos was going to have the great honor of supplying the cedar for Amen's barge, as it had done in the time of his forefathers. The prince pointed out that in the past, Egypt had paid very well for the wood. Then he added, "Amen founded all lands, but he founded first the land of Egypt, for skill and learning came out of it, to reach the place where I am. What then are these silly trips which they have had you make?"

Eventually, after sending back to Egypt for more gold and silver and other trade goods, Wenamen was able to return home to Thebes with fine, seasoned cedar timbers. His troubles along the way, however, show us how far the might and glory of Egypt had declined in the minds of neighbors who only a few generations earlier had been its trembling subjects.

"A BROKEN REED"

A hundred years after Herihor's military coup, a new dynasty took power. These kings were called the Meshwesh, and their origins were in Libya. In fact, they were related to the Sea People whose attempted invasion had been beaten back by the troops of Merneptah, 250 years earlier. The Meshwesh themselves were thoroughly Egyptianized and very proud of the several generations of their ancestors who had lived in the Delta. Even so, this was the first time since the Hyksos invasion that Egypt was ruled by non-Egyptians.

The first pharaoh of the new dynasty was named Sheshonk. He appears in the Bible as Shishak, who led his armies into Palestine and captured Jerusalem during the reign of King Rehoboam. On his return to Egypt, Sheshonk put up a victory gate at Karnak, listing many of the towns he had conquered. Apparently he did not think Jerusalem was very important; it did not make the list.

Sheshonk's invasion of Palestine was only a brief spurt of activity. Afterward, Egypt settled into stagnation. More and more, each separate region went its own way, with occasional intervals of civil war. The country was ripe for picking, but the pickers, when they came, were from an unexpected direction—the south. Nubia and the region called Cush, still farther up the Nile in what is now Sudan, had been part of Egypt all during the New Kingdom. The official known as the King's Son of Cush was usually among the three or four most powerful men in the kingdom.

As Egypt's power dwindled, Cush became independent but stayed faithful to the religion and culture of old Egypt . . . more faithful than the motherland itself. Gradually the king of Cush, Piankhi, extended his rule northward, until even the religious capital of Thebes obeyed him. He donned the double crown, took up the sacred crook and flail, and proclaimed that his father Amen had named him pharaoh.

This would not be so remarkable, except that Piankhi and his fellow Cushites were what the Greeks called Ethiopians. In other words, they were more closely related to black central Africans than to the mostly Semitic people typical of Egypt, Syria, and Libya. This did not make much difference to people of the time. Egyptians were not particularly race-

or color-conscious. They were much too chauvinistic for that. As far as they were concerned, all of humanity was divided into two groups: Egyptians and foreign riffraff. The people of Cush, black or not, were considered to be honorary Egyptians.

Piankhi and his successors did what they could to re-create the Egypt of earlier times. They were meticulous in their worship of Amen-Re and their adherence to the ancient customs. The world, however, had changed. The isolation that had protected the Old and Middle Kingdoms from warlike neighbors was long gone. New powers were taking the world stage. The most important of them was Assyria. When the Assyrian ruler, Sennacherib, attacked the tiny Palestinian kingdoms of Israel and Judah, their chief, Hezekiah, appealed to Egypt for help. The Assyrian leader mocked him for this:

> *Thou trustest upon the staff of this broken reed, even upon Egypt, whereon if a man lean, it will go into his hand and pierce it; so is Pharaoh, king of Egypt, unto all that trust on him.*

According to the account in the Bible, the Assyrians lost that campaign after a plague crippled their army. Soon, however, they were back. After taking care of their lesser foes in Palestine, they continued south and invaded Egypt itself. In 671 BC the Assyrians captured Memphis, the most ancient capital of Egypt, and leveled its legendary walls. Then they loaded their wagons with booty, including the women of the pharaoh's harem, and went home.

Once the Assyrians were out of range, the Cushite pharaoh came north and took power again. The Assyrians returned, under their new king, Asshurbanipal. They won another campaign and left. Again the Cushite army marched north and took power. When the Assyrians returned a third time, they were determined to teach the pesky Egyptians a lesson. The Cushites retreated, first to Thebes, then upriver to their home territory. Asshurbanipal took his revenge on the holy city of Amen. The sack of Thebes became a legend of destruction for generations afterward.

Overextended, Asshurbanipal had to leave a native governor in charge of Egypt. As soon as the Assyrian troops were far enough away, the Egyptian governor rebelled and took power in his own name. His son, Psamtik I, founded the 26th, or Saite, dynasty. One peculiarity of these pharaohs was that they tried to revive the glory of the past by copying it as faithfully as possible. Even experts sometimes have trouble telling a statue or wall painting of the Saite period from its model that is 2,000 years older.

Another feature of the Saite dynasty was its reliance on the support of Greek mercenary troops. As these soldiers finished their service, many of them settled and raised families in the Delta region. Their presence, along with that of the many traders and craftspeople of Greek descent in the Delta cities, gave the region an increasingly un-Egyptian cast. Perhaps the longing for the distant past that shows up in Saite art was a response to this trend *away from* the historical and popular sources of Egyptian culture.

The Assyrians did not return, because they themselves had been conquered by the Babylonians, who in turn fell to the growing Persian empire. In 525 BC the Persian emperor Cambyses made Egypt a province in his empire. With a few intervals of autonomy when the Persians were busy on another front, that status lasted almost 200 years. Egyptians, the people of the Nile Valley, had become the subjects of foreign rulers.

In 332 BC a new conqueror came to Egypt, a young Macedonian named Alexander. He drove out the Persians, then made a pilgrimage to the temple of Amen at the oasis of Siwa. There the oracle proclaimed that Alexander was the divine son of Amen, the true king of Egypt, and the destined king of the world. Alexander apparently took the words of the oracle very seriously. He stayed in Egypt just long enough to found a new capital, Alexandria, in the western Delta and to make one of his generals, Ptolemy, governor. Then he marched away to fulfill the oracle's prediction and conquer the rest of the world. He never returned.

THE LAST PHARAOH

When Alexander died in far-off Persia, in 323 BC, the empire he had put together fell apart. Ptolemy, the Greek general made governor of Egypt, held on to his power and eventually declared himself pharaoh. His descendants ruled Egypt for almost 300 years. Most of them also took the name of Ptolemy, but the most famous of them all, and the last, was named Cleopatra.

It may come as a surprise, but judging by the portraits that have survived, Cleopatra was not a great beauty. However, she obviously had unusual brilliance and charm and a determination that was utterly ruthless. She needed all these qualities. In the end, even they were not enough. The world was changing rapidly. Rome had eliminated its only rival, the North African empire of Carthage, and gone on to conquer Gaul to its north. Now its sights were turning east.

Cleopatra's father, Ptolemy XI, had asked for Roman support after a rebellion chased him from power. That mistake gave Rome a crucial foothold in Egypt. His son, Ptolemy XII, was barely ten when he became king. To make his position more secure, his advisers married him to his 17-year-old sister, Cleopatra. She soon fell out with them, however. She fled to Syria and started assembling an army.

Meanwhile, the first in a series of power struggles had erupted in Rome. Ptolemy was the ward and ally of the loser, Pompey, who took refuge in Alexandria. Ptolemy's advisers had Pompey killed, hoping to gain favor with Pompey's rival, Julius Caesar. This was a bad move. Far from being pleased, Caesar was disgusted by their treachery.

Caesar was also strongly attracted by Cleopatra. The story goes that she got past his guards by having herself carried into his quarters rolled up in a carpet. With Caesar's support, she regained the throne. Not long afterward, her young brother and husband, Ptolemy XII, accidentally drowned in the Nile. She promptly married a still younger brother, who became Ptolemy XIII. Three years later, she had him executed.

Now began the love story that inspired Plutarch and Shakespeare. Julius Caesar was dead, assassinated on the Senate steps in Rome. One of his heirs and avengers was Marc Antony, who came to Egypt to sound Cleopatra's loyalties. He fell hopelessly in love with her and stayed on in Egypt. They were married a few years later, in 36 BC.

Maybe Cleopatra was as passionately in love as Antony; maybe not. What is clear is that she saw in him a weapon she could use to make her kingdom of Egypt a partner of Rome, not just another province of the empire. In this she failed. Civil war broke out between Antony's supporters and those of Octavian, the great-nephew of Julius Caesar who later changed his name to Augustus Caesar. At the sea battle of Actium, in 31 BC, Octavian's navy trounced the combined fleets of Antony and Cleopatra. The two lovers fled to Alexandria, where Antony, according to Roman tradition, fell on his sword.

Cleopatra had one more throw of the dice. When the victorious Octavian arrived in Egypt, she tried her charms on him. It had worked with Julius Caesar and Marc Antony, but it failed this time. Octavian had her locked up. He planned to lead her in chains through the streets of Rome, then stage a public execution. Cleopatra frustrated his plans. According to Plutarch, she bribed a guard to smuggle a basket into her quarters. Inside was a small but deadly cobra. This was the uraeus, the protective symbol worn on the crown of every pharaoh since Narmer, 3,000 years earlier. Now its venom would end the life, but save the dignity, of Egypt's last independent ruler in ancient times.

PART III

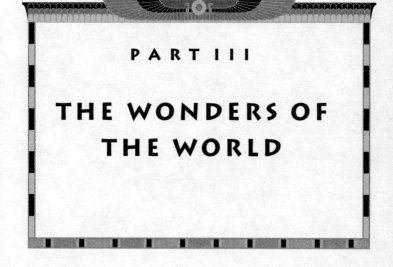

THE WONDERS OF THE WORLD

MOUNTAINS IN STONE

Man fears Time,
But Time fears the Pyramids.
—Arab Proverb

At the edge of the Giza plateau, the shantytown sprawl of Greater Cairo comes to an abrupt stop. Just beyond the line between city and desert, three familiar shapes define the horizon like a scene from a recurring, half-remembered dream. For thousands of years the pyramids of Giza have been the one sight that no visitor to Egypt can ignore. Some go for no other reason but to see them, but even they are seldom prepared for the impact. The unimaginable age and sheer hugeness are more than any photograph or description can communicate.

The Greeks of classical times spoke with awe about the Seven Wonders of the World. These marvels disappeared for a variety of reasons. The 100-foot-tall bronze statue called the Colossus of Rhodes fell during an earthquake around 224 BC; 900 years later, its wreckage was sold as scrap metal. The Pharos, or lighthouse, of Alexandria also lost much of its tower in an earthquake; the stump was finally razed in 1375 AD. The temple of Artemis at Ephesus was destroyed in 262 AD by Goths. The Mausoleum at Halicarnassus was demolished for its marble in 1402 AD. As for the Hanging Gardens of Babylon and the monumental gold and ivory statue of Olympian Zeus, it is not clear exactly when or how they were destroyed, but destroyed, they were.

When Philo of Byzantium compiled his list of the Seven Wonders of the World, around 150 BC, the pyramids of Giza were already over 2,000 years old—far, far older than any of the other Wonders he named. Today they are the only survivors.

A Stairway to Paradise

The pyramids of Egypt did not spring up out of nowhere. They were a logical, if inspired, development from earlier burial customs and religious rites. As we have seen, a person was considered to have a better chance of making a successful journey to the next world if his or her physical body was preserved as a sort of home base for the *ka,* or spiritual double. The *ka* in turn was strengthened by supplies of food, drink, and other necessities of life. These could be literal—actual loaves of bread and jugs of beer—or more symbolic. Models or wall paintings of servants carrying loaves of bread and jugs of beer were almost as good as the real things. It even helped to have someone recite an incantation such as "For the *ka* of So-and-so, a thousand of bread and a thousand of beer."

These beliefs meant that a proper tomb had at least two

important functions. It was a place to keep the person's body in safety, and it was also a place to bring and store the goods needed in the next world. From simple graves with rocks piled on top to keep animals away, the tombs of those who could afford the best expanded both downward and upward. The burial chamber was constructed deeper and deeper in the bedrock, and mastabas were erected on the surface to protect the tomb entrances and provide space for mourning rituals.

The most elaborate tomb, of course, was that of a pharaoh. It was also the most important. This was less because he was the richest or most powerful person in the kingdom, and more because the well-being, even the survival, of the kingdom depended on him. He was a god. If he reached the next world in proper fashion, he would be able to influence the future favorably for his people. If something went wrong, however—and he faced countless dangers on the journey—Egypt would lose forever the benefits of his divine powers.

Around 2630 BC, the pharaoh Djoser asked his vizier, Imhotep, to build him a really impressive tomb in the necropolis of Saqqâra, just west of his capital city of Memphis. Aware of the threat of decay to mud-brick structures, Imhotep decided to build Djoser's new tomb in a new material: dressed stone. Stone had occasionally been used before for the floors of tombs, but until now, no one had attempted to erect an entire building of stone.

Imhotep began to construct a huge mastaba. Pieces of white limestone quarried on the opposite bank of the Nile at Tura were ferried across by boat and painstakingly carved into smooth, regular blocks the size of a traditional mud brick, then set in place. At some point Imhotep decided to enlarge the initial structure by adding onto each side. Because the addition was not as tall as the inner segment, the tomb now looked like a smaller mastaba sitting on top of a larger one.

This accident of design must have given the architect his great inspiration. He placed another, still smaller mastaba on top of the inner structure, then another, smaller yet, on top of that. Now it looked like a four-layer structure. Imhotep and his royal client must have liked the effect, but apparently they thought it was still not quite impressive enough. They decided to make each of the four layers larger on two sides, then add two more layers on top.

The result looked like six mastabas of diminishing size, stacked one on top of another. Because of its silhouette, it became known as the Step Pyramid. The name describes it well, but it also reflects its religious function, as a stairway the pharaoh could climb to his rightful place in heaven.

Djoser's pyramid was big. It rose to a height of 204 feet (62 meters), and its base was 389 by 462 feet (119 × 141 meters), as large as three football fields set side by side. At the time, it was by far the largest building anywhere on earth. And yet it was only one important part of an entire city of the dead. Underground, Imhotep constructed a labyrinth of tunnels, storerooms, galleries, and crypts that is still being explored. Temples and ceremonial courtyards surrounded the pyramid. One small, sealed cubicle on the northeast corner of the pyramid contained an imposing statue of Djoser. Two peepholes allowed the spirit of the god-king to look out toward the polar stars. The statue is now in the Cairo Museum, but visitors can still peer in at a replica of it. The whole complex was encircled by a stone wall over 30 feet high and a mile long, punctuated by thirteen false entrances and one true one.

Several of the pharaohs who came after Djoser in the 3rd dynasty tried to equal the magnificence of his tomb complex. None of them succeeded. Perhaps the problem was that they did not have the help of a mind as inspired as that of Imhotep. Or maybe these projects were left incomplete because the kings who had ordered them died, and their successors decided to put their energy into their own projects instead.

In the desert near the Step Pyramid are the remains of an enclosure as ambitious as Djoser's. It is usually ascribed to the pharaoh Sekhemkhet. The pyramid that was to be its focus never got beyond the second layer. In the maze of subterranean galleries under the unfinished pyramid, archaeologists stumbled across a sealed sarcophagus. A long-withered funeral wreath still rested on top of it.

This was an amazing find—an undisturbed royal burial from the 3rd dynasty! But when the coffin was finally opened, there was nothing inside. Was this a decoy, intended to fool would-be tomb robbers? And if so, is the mummy of Sekhemkhet still hidden elsewhere, in some secret chamber of the complex, along with all the funerary goods of a powerful monarch?

Near Giza are two other 3rd or 4th dynasty tombs where step pyramids were started but never got very far. At one of these sites, known as the "Unfinished Pyramid," a long trench was cut into the rock, leading down to a burial chamber 75 feet (25 meters) below the surface. Inside the chamber was an oval stone sarcophagus, still sealed. When it was opened, it—like that of Sekhemkhet—was empty.

Why would anyone take the trouble to carefully seal and bury an empty sarcophagus? One theory, already mentioned, is that the sealed coffin was meant to fool would-be thieves. But how would that work? Robbers break into a burial chamber, see the sarcophagus . . . and then what? Were they supposed to be so overawed by the sight that they went back the way they came? Not very likely. No, they would break the seals, open the sarcophagus, find out that it was empty, and go on looking for the real one.

We have already gotten acquainted with another explanation, put forward by archaeologist George Reisner, who found the empty sarcophagus of queen Hetepheres in a hastily dug tomb deep underground at Giza. Reisner suggested that the queen's original tomb was invaded by thieves who destroyed her mummy after pillaging it. The official responsible for the tomb's security dreaded the wrath of the king when he learned that his mother's mummy was lost, so he staged a fake reburial.

Reisner's scenario might well explain the particular case of Hetepheres, but what of the other empty coffins? Did the priests and embalmers who were entrusted with the body of a dead god-king routinely lose track of it, like a package gone astray, and have to substitute an empty sarcophagus? That would call for an unbelievable level of carelessness on their part.

There is another possible explanation. What if the burial chambers that have been found inside or under pyramids were never really intended for actual burials? Maybe their function was purely religious and symbolic. If so, it would help explain why *no* royal mummy from the Old Kingdom has been located—they weren't there to start with. Of course, the theory does not tell us where the mummies *were* buried, or why, but after all, we do not expect to find the body of Washington under the Washington Monument or the body of Lincoln inside the Lincoln Memorial.

From Stepped to Smooth

Forty miles south of Memphis, at Meidum, an immense steep-sided stone structure towers over a bluff at the desert's edge. This is the central core, all that's left, of the pyramid of Huni, the last pharaoh of the 3rd dynasty. What he built on the site was an eight-layer step pyramid, the first to be completed since Djoser's. His successor (who was probably also his son), Snefru, then took a radical new direction. He had each of the huge steps filled with rubble, then faced the structure with blocks of smooth limestone to create a continuous slope on each side. The result was Egypt's first true pyramid. When completed, it was over 300 feet (92 meters) tall and 470 feet (144 meters) on each side. In later centuries, the valuable casing stones were stripped away, leaving the exposed core we see today.

What was behind the change from stepped to smooth-sided pyramids? Some scholars believe this shift reflected the growing influence of the cult of the sun-god Re. As we have seen, a living pharaoh was believed to be the embodiment of the god Horus. On his death, he was translated to the stars as the god Osiris/Orion. The step pyramid had the same form as the hieroglyph for "ladder" (or maybe the hieroglyph took its form from the pyramid), and it is reasonable to see the tomb as a ladder to the stars.

Over the course of the Old Kingdom, however, the idea began to take hold that the king was the son of Re (an idea that gave the priests of Re a more important role in the kingdom). After death, he was taken up into the barque of the sun. Did the form of the true pyramid remind people of the triangular pattern sunbeams make when they shine through a break in clouds? If so, the smooth sides could have seemed a continuation of the rays. In addition, the pyramid was similar in shape to the *benben*. This was the conical stone, perhaps an iron-rich meteorite, that stood in the courtyard of the temple of Re in Heliopolis. It was considered one of the holiest objects in Egypt. One thing is certain: Under the bright sunlight of the desert, a pyramid clad all in white limestone was a dazzling sight, worthy to be the earthly resting place of a son of the sun.

Having completed his father's pyramid, Snefru went on to build, not one, but two more true pyramids for himself. Both are at Dahshur, a few miles south of Saqqâra. Why two? No one knows. There may be a clue to the reason in the name of one of them. It's called the Bent Pyramid. The walls of this very distinctive structure start off at a steeper slope than the earlier pyramid at Meidum—54° 31' versus 51° 53'. Halfway up, however, the sides angle inward to a much gentler slope of 43° 21'. Did the builders run into problems attaching the limestone casing stones to the steep sides?

Its silhouette is not the only odd feature of the Bent Pyramid. It also has two entrances, each leading to a different burial chamber. Was either chamber ever used? That is another unanswered question. Even stranger, when archaeologists first explored the pyramid in the early years of the 19th century, they reported a very peculiar incident. Suddenly a cold wind swept through the corridors, so strong that it almost blew out their lanterns. After a couple of days, it stopped, and they never figured out where it had come from. Are there hidden passages and chambers still to be found within or beneath the Bent Pyramid? If so, what new discoveries might they hold?

Snefru's other pyramid is called the Red Pyramid because of its facing stones of reddish limestone. Its slope is only 43° 36'. This is almost identical to the slope of the upper half of the Bent Pyramid. Some authorities believe the Red Pyramid was built first and that its gentle slope reflects the hesitancy and caution of the builders. Others hold that Snefru was unhappy with the Bent Pyramid's bentness and built the Red Pyramid as a substitute. There are also some who feel that he intended to build both pyramids from the beginning and chose their sites in accord with mystical religious considerations.

The two pyramids at Dahshur are very large. Each is just over 340 feet (100 meters) tall, about the height of a 30-story building. The Bent Pyramid is 620 feet (189 meters) on a side. The Red Pyramid, because of its gentler overall slope, is even larger, 840 feet (220 meters) on a side. Together they weigh in the neighborhood of nine million tons. When we consider that Snefru also completed the pyramid at Meidum, he seems a shoo-in for the title of champion pyramid builder of all time. However, Snefru had a son who became pharaoh after him. The son's name was Khufu. In later centuries the Greeks would know him as Cheops.

"The Great Despot"

> *Cheops succeeded to the throne and plunged into all manner of wickedness. He closed the temples, and forbade the Egyptians to offer sacrifice, compelling them instead to labor, one and all, in his service . . . One hundred thousand men labored constantly, and were relieved every three months by a fresh lot. It took ten years' oppression of the people to make the causeway for the conveyance of the stones . . . The pyramid itself was twenty years in building. (Herodotus)*

We can all visualize the scene: the long lines of sweating, half-starved, half-naked slaves leaning far forward to haul the enormous blocks of stone, the sneering overseers whipping them on, and in the background, Pharaoh and his court reclining indolently on bright cushions and sipping . . . well, not Chardonnay or even lemonade, but something at least as decadent. The image owes a lot to Hollywood, of course, but Hollywood owes it, ultimately, to Herodotus. And why not? Didn't he go to Egypt in person? What better evidence could anyone ask for?

Herodotus *did* go to Egypt. While he was there, he asked a lot of questions about Egyptian history and culture. Later he wrote down the answers. He is by far the oldest non-Egyptian source we have on the subject. Unfortunately, he is not the most reliable. The people he questioned, whom he took to be learned priests, were apparently dragomans, freelance guides. Like their descendants today who rent camels and donkeys to tourists, they were full of colorful stories that probably got more colorful with each retelling. Herodotus lapped them up.

One story he loved, and retold quite indignantly, was the one about Pharaoh's daughter. It is worth quoting:

> *The wickedness of Cheops reached to such a pitch that, when he had spent all his treasures and wanted more, he sent his daughter to the stews [brothels], with orders to procure him a certain sum—how much I cannot say, for I was not told; she procured it, however, and at the same time, bent on leaving a monument which should perpetuate her own memory, she required each man who sought intercourse to make her a present of a stone toward the works which she contemplated. With these stones she built the pyramid which stands midmost of the three that are in front of the great pyramid, measuring along each side 150 feet.*

If each stone was three feet on a side, that's 2,500 stones just in the bottom layer. By the time the poor princess reached the eighth layer, she would have needed about 15,000 customers, or three a night for 14 years, and her pyramid would still be only 24 feet tall, barely a pimple on the face of the Giza plateau. It is hard to understand how Herodotus managed to take this nonsense seriously.

A point to keep in mind is that Herodotus visited Egypt around 450 BC. A long time ago, yes, but that was already *more than 2,000 years* after the pyramids were built. Put another way, if you drew a time line linking our age and the Age of Pyramids, Herodotus would fall close to the halfway point. Imagine visiting Rome and asking a passerby about a 2,000-year-old monument such as the Colosseum. Who built it, and how and why? You might hear some reasonably accurate information. You would certainly hear all sorts of tall tales and legends. And you would have no way of knowing which parts were which.

In any case, Herodotus can be forgiven his befuddlement. Khufu's pyramid and its two near neighbors have that effect on people. It is not simply their immensity. Even in their present dilapidated state, they also give the impression of incredible precision. The gigantic blocks of stone are fitted so exactly that a credit card can't be inserted between them. This, more than the sheer size of the Giza pyramids, has given rise to the wildest theories about their origin and purpose. Anyone with enough time and manpower can pile up an enormous heap of stones. But to cut millions of stones to such precise sizes and shapes, then place them exactly where they have to go, calls for technical and organizational skills that seem almost superhuman.

The Great Pyramid was originally 482 feet (146 meters) tall, or about one and a half times the height of the Statue of Liberty. Over the centuries it has lost its capstone and top few courses of stones, along with all its casing stones, bringing it down to 451 feet (137 meters). Each side is 756 feet (230 meters) long; the base is so close to being a perfect square that the difference between the longest side, on the south, and the shortest, on the north, is less than eight inches.

The base is also amazingly close to being perfectly level. The difference in height between the lowest and highest corner is only half an inch. Considering that the area of the base is over 13 acres (over 54,000 square meters), this is precision indeed. The orientation is just as precise; the four sides line up almost perfectly with true north, south, east, and west.

How did the architects of the Old Kingdom manage to work to such exactness, using nothing more complicated than knotted cords, plumb bobs, wooden squares, and copper tools? Archaeologists believe they did it by relying on what they knew very well—the stars and water. The rising and setting points of stars that circle the North Star would have given them a very precise measure of true north. A network of narrow trenches filled with water would have allowed them to level the site of the new pyramid, again with great precision. Afterward, the trenches could be filled in.

The stones that made up the core of the pyramid—more than two million of them, weighing about two and a half tons apiece—were quarried nearby. Only the fine white limestone for the casing blocks had to be ferried across from Tura, on the other side of the river. Once on the building site, the stones were cut to size with copper saws and chisels, then moved into place. Access ramps of rubble or mud brick were probably built along each side of the pyramid, winding upward around it as it grew.

Recent experiments have shown that dragging a heavy stone block up a track of damp clay is much easier than researchers had expected. Herodotus said that 100,000 men worked on the pyramid. Egyptologist Mark Lehner now suspects that the job could have been done with as few as 10,000. Of these, perhaps 4,000 would have been a permanent team of skilled craftsmen. The rest were probably peasants who worked on the project during the months when the annual Nile flood made farming impossible. In recent years, Lehner and other researchers have uncovered traces at Giza of buildings where pyramid workers lived, cemeteries where they were buried, and even a bakery and brewery that served as their commissary.

The interior passages and chambers of Khufu's pyramid were constructed as the pyramid was going up. They show that the plans went through some radical changes. The tradition since the days of mastabas was to place the burial chamber deep underground. Khufu's pyramid has such a chamber, quarried from the bedrock directly under the center of the pyramid. From the pyramid's entrance high on the north side, a slanting corridor 350 feet long leads down through the stones of the pyramid, then tunnels through bedrock to the chamber. The walls and floor of the underground chamber are still unfinished. Apparently it was abandoned in midproject.

A second burial chamber was built inside the pyramid, not far above ground level. It is now known (mistakenly) as the Queen's Chamber. This, too, was left unfinished when the plans apparently changed again. Another burial chamber, the King's Chamber, was then constructed at a higher level. A long, narrow passage with a corbeled ceiling 28 feet (8.5 meters) high leads steeply up to it. This passage, the Grand Gallery, is one of the most impressive spaces in all of Egypt. Inside the King's Chamber is an enormous sarcophagus—empty, of course. The granite for it was brought 400 miles downriver from the quarries at Aswan, and it was lowered into the chamber before the ceiling of stacked granite slabs was put in place. Each of those slabs weighs over 40 tons.

Once the pyramid-shaped capstone was placed at the apex of the pyramid, the builders began dismantling the winding ramps. At the same time they smoothed and polished the limestone facing blocks, starting from the top down. This is what Herodotus must have meant by a statement that has puzzled readers for centuries: "The upper portion of the pyramid was finished first, then the middle, and finally the part which was lowest and nearest the ground." Once the last ramp was taken down, the pyramid shone forth in all its majesty.

But not alone. An Old Kingdom pyramid stood at the center of a complex of structures. These became so standardized that an archaeologist who uncovers one element of an Old Kingdom pyramid complex can point confidently to where the others must lie buried beneath the sand.

At the boundary between desert and cultivated land stood the valley temple, often linked to the river by a canal. During construction, this was where boats landed the gigantic blocks of granite and limestone. Later, when the king died, the royal funeral barge brought his body here to be purified and mummified. This was also the site of the religious ceremony called the Opening of the Mouth. Priests, worshipers, and members of the pharaoh's family placed the mummy near life-size statues of the king, anointed it, and touched it with sacred metal tools. This ceremony joined the body spiritually to the statues; as long as even one of them lasted, the king's soul would have an earthly home. The ceremony also gave back the power of speech, so that the pharaoh would be able to speak the appropriate prayers and spells on his journey to the next world.

Afterward, the royal coffin was carried through a long, covered stone causeway that stretched from the valley temple to a second temple that was built against the eastern face of the pyramid. After the mummy was placed in its sarcophagus inside the pyramid (or wherever it was in fact placed), this second or mortuary temple became the center of the transfigured god-king's cult. Here priests offered daily meals to his *ka,* and worshipers prayed for advice and help.

Another element in this city of the dead was one or more much smaller satellite pyramids. The three of these near the southeast corner of Khufu's pyramid are thought to have been built as tombs for his three queens. Nearby are boat pits where the barges used in the funeral were entombed for the pharaoh's use in the afterlife. One of Khufu's royal barges was recently dug up and reconstructed after 4,500 years underground. At least one more is still there in its stone-lined pit. Rows of mastaba tombs built for the pharaoh's courtiers and high officials complete the pyramid complex.

A PATH TO THE STARS

As far back as the 17th century, people exploring the King's Chamber of the Great Pyramid noticed two small shafts leading up at a slant from opposite sides of the room. Experiments with smoky fires proved that these shafts went all the way through the pyramid to the outside. Only nine inches (22 centimeters) on a side, they were much too small to serve as passages, so it was decided that they must have been air shafts. While it was true that no other pyramid had ventilating shafts leading to the burial chamber, no other pyramid had such an elaborate interior either.

In the 1870s an English engineer named Waynman Dixon went hunting for similar air shafts in the Queen's Chamber. Armed with hammers and steel chisels, he found two shafts hidden behind the limestone walls. However, just as these new shafts had not opened into the room, they also did not penetrate to the outside. The accepted explanation for this oddity was that construction must have stopped on them when the Queen's Chamber was abandoned.

Making these shafts was a very complicated and tedious process. They were not drilled through the solid masonry;

the Egyptians had no tools to do a job like that. Instead, as the pyramid rose, each massive block that was about to be set in the path of a shaft had to have its section of the channel carved through it. No commonplace purpose would have justified that level of effort and exactness.

In the 1920s experts began suggesting that the function of the shafts was not practical but religious—not to let in air, but to let out the soul of the buried king. This theory received a boost when Egyptologist Alexander Badawy and astronomer Virginia Trimble discovered that the northern shaft from the King's Chamber points directly at the location around 2500 BC of the star Alpha Draconis, which was then the North Star. The southern shaft points just as directly at the ancient path of the three brightest stars in the constellation Orion, which the Egyptians called Sahu and identified with Osiris. As for the partial shaft on the southern side of the Queen's Chamber, it has been shown to point to the ancient location of Sirius. This star's reappearance above the horizon signaled the annual Nile flood. Sirius was closely identified with Isis, in part because of the myth that the Nile flood was caused by Isis weeping for dead Osiris. The shafts, then, gave the pharaoh's *ka* connections to both Isis and Osiris, as well as to the northern stars known as "the Imperishable Ones."

Recently author Robert Bauval has suggested that the links between the pyramids and the stars were even more extensive. He points out that the Great Pyramid and its closest neighbor, the pyramid of Khafre, have their diagonals on almost exactly the same line. However, the third pyramid at Giza, that of Menkaure, is offset slightly to the east. The pattern they form on the ground is very similar to the pattern the three stars of Orion's Belt form in the sky. Bauval does not think this is a coincidence. Instead it is an expression of the mystical principle "On earth as it is in heaven." The pharaohs did not build the pyramids out of vanity, as monuments to their own glory. These great structures were a celebration and an illustration of their religious beliefs, just as the great cathedrals of Europe were a celebration and an illustration of the beliefs of medieval Christianity.

Khufu's pyramid was the largest ever built, but it was not the last. His successors, Khafre and Menkaure, built theirs near his on the Giza plateau. Khafre's pyramid is 471 feet (143 meters) tall and 707 feet (215 meters) square, or slightly smaller than Khufu's pyramid. It gives the impression of being larger, partly because it is built on slightly higher ground and partly because it still retains some of its limestone casing near the summit.

Other pharaohs of the 4th and 5th dynasties built their pyramids closer to Memphis, at Saqqâra and Abusir. As time went on, the workmanship grew more and more sloppy. Architects realized that they could put up a pyramid more quickly and cheaply by building slanted stone walls around the perimeter and filling the center with rubble and sand. Once the structure was encased in white limestone, it looked just as impressive as earlier pyramids with their solid masonry cores. Later, however, as the casing stones were stolen for reuse, these shoddy constructions settled into unimpressive piles of gravel. Some eroded away entirely, leaving only a buried foundation as evidence that they had ever existed.

One late pyramid that still draws visitors is at Saqqâra, practically next door to the Step Pyramid of Djoser. It was built for Unis, the last pharaoh of the 5th dynasty. The exterior is not impressive, but the attraction is inside. The walls of the burial chamber and anteroom are covered with carved hieroglyphic inscriptions. These make up the earliest known version of what are called the "Pyramid Texts." This was a collection of prayers, magical spells, and incantations intended to guide and protect the spirit of the dead king on its way to the afterlife. In later dynasties, many of these ancient texts would find their way into the scrolls that have come to be known as the Book of the Dead.

The God's Request

It was a warm afternoon. The prince had been tracking a lion for hours, leaving his companions far behind. The trail had brought him to a holy place from the old days, known as the Horizon of Khufu. Ranging on his left were the three mountains, each joined to its valley temple by a causeway of massive stones. Next to the second of the three temples, a gigantic head of stone protruded from the sand. Its Osiris beard and the cobra on its headdress marked it as a god-king. The prince knew its name: *Hor-am-Akhet,* Horus in the Horizon. As he saluted it, he noticed an attractive patch of shade on the north side of the head. The sight reminded him of how tired he was. He lay down on the sand, pillowed his head on his arm, and fell asleep.

When he awoke, he remembered that the god had spoken to him in a dream. The drifting sands had all but buried the god and robbed him of his glory. If the young prince would clear away the sand and restore the great statue to its original beauty, his reward would be the Horus Throne itself, even if he was not first in the succession. The prince eagerly accepted the bargain. He set men to work uncovering the lion body and paws of the god. A thousand years of windblown sand had not been kind to the statue, so he encased the eroded parts in blocks of limestone. As a final touch, he painted the god's face bright red, his body and forelegs yellow, and his royal headdress blue.

Horus in the Horizon kept his word. Around 1400 BC, following the death of his father, the prince rose to become the pharaoh Thutmose IV. The texts do not say what happened to his older brother, the legitimate heir. Thutmose ordered the story of his dream inscribed on a 12-foot-tall red granite stela. This was set up between the front paws of the god and later enclosed in a chapel. The chapel and its stela were uncovered 3,200 years later, in 1818 AD, by an Italian treasure hunter named Giovanni Caviglia. By now, the gigantic statue was once again buried up to the neck in sand, and its name had changed. No longer Horus in the Horizon, it was now known as the Great Sphinx.

The Sphinx had been "born" close to 1,000 years before Thutmose IV restored it. The crews that built the Great Pyramid of Khufu had quarried most of the stone for the central core nearby, at the edge of the Giza plateau. In the middle of one U-shaped quarry, they had left behind a rocky knoll of limestone. A generation later, Khafre began work on his pyramid, just to the south of Khufu's. The large, unsightly outcropping stood barely a hundred yards from the site of his valley temple and right next to the path of the causeway from the temple to the new pyramid. It would have to be dealt with.

At that point someone must have noticed that the knoll looked like a crouching animal. Egyptians were accustomed to images of gods that were part human and part animal. The next step was not that difficult for them. Instead of leveling the outcropping, why not carve it into the form of a monumental guardian for the pharaoh's pyramid? For its body, the lion, symbol of strength and courage, and for the head, an idealized pharaoh, perhaps based on Khafre himself.

The statue they carved is monumental indeed—240 feet (73 meters) long and 66 feet (20 meters) high. The lips on the huge face are seven feet across, and the nose is almost six feet high. Or rather, it was when it was still there. In 1300 AD a zealous Moslem official, Sheik Mohammed, became upset that the local people still venerated the Sphinx. To show that it was not holy, he chiseled off the nose, the beard, and the sacred cobra on its headdress. A story is still repeated that in 1798 Napoleon's cannoneers used the Sphinx for target practice. This is a myth. The damage the French soldiers were supposed to have caused had already been done hundreds of years earlier.

In Egyptian, one of the names for the great statue was *Seshep-Ankh,* or "Eternal Image." When the Greeks arrived in Egypt centuries later, they apparently heard this word as *sphinx,* or "strangler." In Greek mythology this is the name of a ferocious creature with the head of a woman and the body of a bird. The Greeks extended this name to the statue of Horus in the Horizon, as well as to other Egyptian figures with animal bodies and human heads.

Later, after the Moslem conquest in 700 AD, there was another misunderstanding over names. When the Arab newcomers pointed to the Sphinx and asked, "What is that?" the natives told them, "*Per-Hol,* the Place of Hol [a corrupted name for Horus]." The Arabs misheard *hol* as the Arabic word for overwhelming fear. As a result, to this day Egyptians and other speakers of Arabic refer to the Sphinx as *Abu Hol,* the Father of Terror.

Like the uraeus, the royal cobra on the pharaoh's crown, the Sphinx was meant to be frightening, but only to evildoers. It was the guardian of the entire pyramid complex. On a stela from Khafre's time, the Sphinx says:

> *. . . I protect the chapel of thy tomb. I guard thy sepulchral chamber. I ward off the intruding stranger. I hurl the foes to the ground and their weapons with them. I drive away the wicked one from the chapel of thy tomb. I destroy thine adversaries in their lurking place . . .*

From the time it was completed, the Sphinx was given divine honors. A temple was built in Khafre's time facing the Sphinx's paws. Little remains of the Sphinx Temple today, but that little shows it was built of gigantic stone blocks, much bigger than the ones used to build the pyramids. Many weighed 50 tons, and a few monsters may have weighed as much as 200 tons. How these stones were transported and set in place is a mystery. Another mystery is *why* the builders chose to use these enormous megaliths. Was it meant as a gesture of respect to the Sphinx, which is carved from the solid stone of Earth itself?

Like the neighboring pyramids, the Sphinx is meticulously aligned. Its gaze points directly east, toward the exact point on the horizon where the sun rises on the first day of spring. Scholars believe that this orientation was meant to symbolize the pharaoh, in his embodiment as Horus, saluting the sun god Re.

An ancient monument as imposing and mysterious as the Sphinx is bound to give rise to folk tales and legends. One of the most persistent is that there are secret passages and chambers within or beneath the Sphinx. In Roman days it was believed that a hidden stair led up into a room inside the head. From there the priests could speak messages that appeared to come from the god.

In more modern times, mystics, occultists, and groups as varied as Rosicrucians, Freemasons, and Theosophists have held that the Sphinx is the true entrance to the Great Pyramid. One account claims that between the paws of the Sphinx there is a set of bronze doors only a master can see and open. Behind the doors, a secret stairway leads to an underground temple. Neophytes were brought here, then taken into a maze of buried passages that symbolized the paths of wisdom. Those who found their way to the ceremonial chamber at the far end were worthy to be initiated into the mysteries. A recent best-selling book even provides maps that show a hidden chamber deep beneath the Sphinx. The authors suggest that this chamber holds the secret of eternal life, concealed there 12,000 years ago by refugees from the lost continent of Atlantis.

Throughout their history, the Egyptians went underground, deep into the bedrock, to build their most important tombs. The King's Chamber, in the center of the Great Pyramid, is a rare exception to this rule. To protect these underground tombs against intruders, the builders used a fiendish assortment of trapdoors, blind alleys, concealed shafts, false entrances, hidden chambers, and bewildering passages. The only tombs we know about are the ones where these deceptive techniques failed. First, robbers discovered ways around them. Later, archaeologists followed the lead of the robbers.

Are there other underground complexes still under the rocks and sand? Almost certainly. And it is quite possible that one of them is in the neighborhood of the Sphinx. A lot of researchers have thought it was worth their while to look. So far, however, the latest seismic, radar, and electromagnetic techniques have failed to turn up any evidence of unknown tunnels and rooms under the Sphinx. Some cavities have shown up—one Egyptologist describes the limestone under the Sphinx as resembling Swiss cheese—but when researchers drilled down into them, they found nothing manmade.

All the talk about secret temples under the Sphinx has diverted attention from the condition of the monument itself. Simply put, the Sphinx is in a bad way. The part of the knoll that became the head was high-quality stone that is still in reasonably good shape. However, the limestone of the middle parts of the body is flaky, almost powdery. Windblown sand has been eroding it for thousands of years, and it shows.

More recently, pollution from Cairo—now a megalopolis of more than 17 million people—has also taken a toll. Raw sewage from nearby slums seeps into the base of the Sphinx and corrodes it. The smog, among the heaviest in the world, eats away at the surface. Restoration projects, from the time of Thutmose IV to our own, often do more damage than they repair.

Photos taken only 20 or 30 years ago show how much detail in the carving is being lost from month to month. This raises a horrible possibility. A day may come, not long from now, when the Sphinx will once again be what it was before the time of Khafre—a limestone outcropping that faintly resembles a crouching animal.

A GOD FALLS SILENT

Tourists have been visiting the monuments of Egypt for thousands of years. They have come to see the pyramids and the Sphinx, of course, but there are also other celebrated sights farther upriver. In the autumn of the year 130 AD, the Roman emperor Hadrian paid a state visit to his province of Egypt. His empress, Sabina, accompanied him. Their entourage included an aristocratic poet named Julia Balbilla, who memorialized the events of the trip in graceful Latin verse. In mid-November, the group sailed up the Nile to Thebes, the ancient capital. They probably visited all the notable sites, but the destination they were most eager to see was in a low-lying field on the west bank of the river. There, two colossal seated figures, weighing 750 tons apiece, stared blindly across the landscape. The one to the north was in sad shape; its top half had tumbled down centuries before.

The Romans, like the Greeks before them, thought these were statues of the hero Memnon. According to Homer, Memnon was the son of the dawn goddess Aurora. He fought in the Trojan War and was made immortal after being killed by Achilles. The reason for this identification was also the reason a visit to the colossi was a must: At dawn, the northern statue spoke. At any rate, it made a noise. Some witnesses thought it was a twang like the sound of a breaking harp string. Others were positive it was a human voice, though they could not make out the words.

Surely this was the voice of Memnon saluting his divine mother, Aurora. Those who heard it were very impressed.

So before dawn on November 19, 130 AD, the emperor Hadrian, the empress Sabina, and all their courtiers waited on the plain of Memnon. Throngs of priests and local officials surrounded them. The sun rose above the horizon and reddened the gigantic statue. The crowd listened breathlessly.

Memnon had nothing to say that day.

The priests and officials who were Hadrian's hosts must have been mortified. They may have been terrified as well. Roman emperors were not used to being slighted, even by the effigy of an immortal.

The next morning, the empress went back. Her poet friend, Julia Balbilla, accompanied her and gave the statue a talking-to:

> *You who are the son of Aurora, O Memnon, and of the venerable Tithonus, you who sit before the Theban city of Zeus—or you, Amenoth, Egyptian king, as the priests declare who are versed in ancient lore—receive my salutation, and by singing, welcome in your turn the revered wife of Emperor Hadrian . . .*

Yesterday, O Memnon, you received the royal pair in silence, so that lovely Sabina would be forced to return, for you were charmed by the gracious beauty of our Queen. Pray give a divine cry when she comes, lest the Emperor be angry with you; too long you have dared to keep her waiting, his august and lawful wife.

Apparently the poet's threats worked:

Then Memnon, in dread of great Hadrian's might, let forth a sudden cry that she heard with joy . . . It was as if one struck a copper gong, and Memnon once more gave a piercing cry as a salute. Even a third time he made a sound.

Then Emperor Hadrian himself lavished salutations upon Memnon, and on the stone he left these verses for posterity, to tell of all he saw and heard.

The verses of Julia Balbilla can still be seen, carved onto the left leg of the mighty statue.

The "priests . . . who are versed in ancient lore" were quite right, by the way. The two colossi have nothing to do with Memnon. They are statues of the 18th dynasty pharaoh Amenhotep III ("Amenoth"), often called Amenhotep the Magnificent. They originally stood as guardians on either side of the great door to his mortuary temple, built around 1360 BC. Their size gives us an idea of the scale of the temple. It is the best idea we are likely to get; generation after generation used Amenhotep's temple as a handy source of cut stone. Long before Hadrian's time, it had vanished altogether, leaving only the two huge seated figures mysteriously alone in a field.

Some 70 years after the visit of Hadrian, Sabina, and Julia Balbilla, another Roman emperor, Septimus Severus, came to pay his respects to Memnon. This time, too, the immortal hero kept quiet. The emperor decided that Memnon must be brooding over the damaged state of his statue. He ordered sculptors and stonemasons to restore the body and head. They did a good job. It is still holding together 1,800 years later. However, their efforts must have interfered with the peculiar configuration of the stones that had given Memnon his voice. He has been silent ever since.

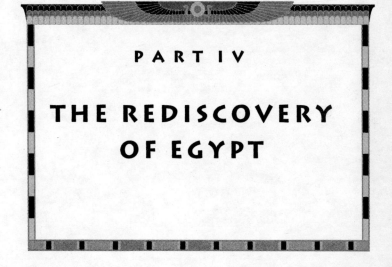

PART IV

THE REDISCOVERY OF EGYPT

THE KEY TO A FORGOTTEN WORLD

After the death of Cleopatra, in 30 BC, Egypt became a province first in the Roman Empire, then in its successor in the East, the Byzantine Empire. In 642 AD Arab armies captured Alexandria from the Byzantines. The dominant religion of the country shifted from Coptic Christianity to Islam, and the Christian world lost touch with the region. In the 16th century Egypt was conquered by the Ottoman Turks, who appointed local officials called pashas to govern the province, with the support of a group of hereditary warriors called Mamelukes.

In the summer of 1798, Napoleon Bonaparte landed in Egypt at the head of a French army. He was not yet emperor, but at 29 he was already the most renowned and successful general in the ranks of the French Republic. He had come to Egypt with two goals. By far the most important to him was to distract France's enemies, the English, by threatening their rich colonies in the East. At the same time he hoped to learn as much as possible about the ancient Egyptians.

In Napoleon's day, the civilization that had flourished along the Nile two millennia before was known to Europeans only by some intriguing accounts in the Bible and classical literature and by the overwhelming monuments it had left behind. Who were the Egyptians? How had they lived? What beliefs had led them to mummify their dead and build great tombs to guard them? No one really knew. To answer these questions and a host of others, Napoleon recruited a corps of more than 160 scholars, artists, and scientists to accompany his army. The mission they were given was not modest: to learn everything they could about Egypt's history and culture.

The French invasion of Egypt began brilliantly. Napoleon captured Alexandria on July 1. He then went on to defeat the fierce Mamelukes at the Battle of the Pyramids. As his victorious armies marched past in review, he exclaimed, "Soldiers! Forty centuries look down upon you!" (Or at least, that's the way he recalled the event when he was writing his memoirs.)

Once in Cairo, Napoleon took over a palace and declared it the headquarters of *l'Institut d'Égypte,* the Egyptian Institute. His team of scholars moved in and went straight to work. Only days later, on August 1, an English fleet commanded by Horatio Nelson surprised the French fleet at anchor in Abukir harbor and totally destroyed it. Having just conquered the land, the French were suddenly stranded there.

For the next year, Napoleon's soldiers fought off attacks by the English, their Turkish allies, and a guerrilla force of Mameluke cavalry. Meanwhile, the scholars of the Institute went on with their mission. They clambered to the tops of monuments with measuring rods. They gathered and cataloged specimens of plants, insects, birds, and animals. They made careful, detailed copies of the paintings and hieroglyphic inscriptions they found on the walls of temples and tombs. Theirs was not a very safe occupation. They were working in a war zone.

Photography had not yet been invented. That meant the artists of the Institute had a very special role. Their records of the art and architecture of Egypt would make it possible for the first time for people in Europe to become acquainted with the ancient culture of the Nile. One of the most dedicated and gifted of these artists was Dominique-Vivant Denon. He was also one of the most daring. When a detachment of the army went south in pursuit of the Mamelukes, Denon went along. For the next ten months, he drew the temple of Karnak, the ruins of Thebes, the tombs in the Valley of the Kings, the temples on the island of Philae . . . Sometimes he became so engrossed in his work that he stayed at his easel while the army marched on. If someone hadn't been sent back for him, he would have found himself alone in the desert.

Denon returned to Cairo with a portfolio crammed full of drawings. He would later use these as the basis for the engravings in his classic book, *Travels in Upper and Lower Egypt.* They clearly showed what all the scholars of the Institute already realized. Ancient Egypt had been a mighty, subtle, and incredibly resilient civilization with an immensely long and complex history. But what *was* that history? The only way they would be able to answer that question was if they first solved what seemed an impossible problem—learning to read hieroglyphs.

Scholars and mystics had been trying to make sense of hieroglyphic inscriptions for more than 1,500 years, since early in the Christian era when the last temples of the old

Egyptian gods were shut down. Some were certain they had succeeded. Unfortunately, the translations they published owed everything to their imaginations and nothing to the actual meaning of the Egyptian text.

All of them started with the same assumption. Since the little drawings were obviously of objects—a basket, a seated man, an owl, a snake—each one must stand for a particular word or concept. Seeing the symbol of a lion, for example, the would-be translator reasoned that it must stand for some lionlike quality, such as courage or kingliness.

This was not such a far-fetched idea. Chinese writing had an ideogram for each word. Why not ancient Egyptian? This supposed similarity between ancient Egyptian and Chinese gave rise to even wilder suppositions. One 18th-century French scholar decided it was evidence that China had been settled many centuries earlier by Egyptians. English scholars disagreed. They argued that ancient Egypt must have been settled by Chinese.

Napoleon's team of savants was too busy accumulating knowledge to be distracted by arguments of this sort. As for Napoleon himself, he was more concerned with finding a way out of the trap he had landed himself in. After beating back an attempt by a Turkish force to land at Abukir, he and a handful of aides managed to slip through the British naval blockade and return to France. His army was left to fend for itself. Desperate, the French troops began to strengthen their lines and wait for the inevitable assault.

In August 1799 a detachment was digging trenches near the ruins of an old fort outside the port town of Rosetta, some 35 miles north of Alexandria. Their commander was an officer of engineers, Major Pierre Bouchard. One of the work crews called Bouchard over. They had just uncovered something interesting. It was a big slab of polished black stone, about three and a half feet high by two and a half feet across. Three of the corners were broken off, giving it something close to an oval shape. Its face was covered with carved characters. The major examined it with mounting excitement.

Across the top part of the slab were fourteen lines of hieroglyphs. The bottom third was covered with closely spaced lines of Greek characters. The middle section was in a script that looked completely unfamiliar. Bouchard knew the directive, issued by General Bonaparte himself. Any object of historical importance was to be forwarded at once to the Institute in Cairo. This certainly fit that description. He ordered his men to search the area for any other stone fragments with writing on them. None turned up, so Bouchard passed the slab on to his superior, General Menou, who sent it, carefully wrapped, to Cairo. Then Bouchard turned his mind back to the job of fortifying his position.

The moment the experts of the Institute examined the stone, they realized they had one of the greatest archaeological finds in history. The reason was set forth in the last section of the passage in Greek:

> *This decree shall be inscribed on a stela of hard stone in sacred and native and Greek characters . . .*

"Sacred" obviously referred to the hieroglyphs, and "native" to the unknown script in the center section. The scholars decided that must be what Herodotus had called demotic, or popular. The passage confirmed what they had hardly dared to hope. The three sections of the stone contained the *same text, but in different languages and systems of writing.* The slab of black basalt, soon known throughout the world as the Rosetta Stone, was nothing less than the key to the language, history, and culture of ancient Egypt.

However, like any key that has been lying around unused for a great many years, it did not turn easily.

The 18th century in Western Europe was a time when every schoolboy was expected to know ancient Greek. It was child's play to transcribe and translate the Greek version. This turned out to be the text of a decree issued in 196 BC by the assembled priests of Egypt. It praised the new pharaoh, 13-year-old Ptolemy V, for his generosity to the gods and ordered that his statue be set up in every important temple and given divine honors. Once the equivalent words were located in the two other versions, the mystery of the hieroglyphs would be a mystery no longer.

This was not nearly as simple as it sounded. Not only was the writing of ancient Egypt unknown, so was the language. The only reason the task was not completely impossible was that Coptic Christians had preserved a language that descended from Egyptian, although it was written in Greek characters. By working backward from a Coptic word, a linguist could make an educated guess about the form of the corresponding word in Egyptian.

The French scholars of the Egyptian Institute did not have the time or the serenity to attack this problem. British troops landed near Alexandria in early 1801. A couple of months later, Cairo fell to a Turkish army. The Institute, its scholars, and all the materials they had accumulated over three years were evacuated to Alexandria. Finally, in September 1801, the weary and outnumbered French army surrendered to the British.

The general commanding the British forces announced that he was going to seize all the documents and specimens the French scholars had collected. Faced with their outraged protests, he backed down. On one point, though, he would not budge. The Rosetta Stone now belonged to Britain. A few months later, after an ocean voyage from Alexandria to London, it was given a place of honor in the British Museum. It may still be seen there today.

The French had had the foresight to copy the Rosetta Stone while they still controlled it. They had done this by treating it as a lithographic plate: They inked it completely, wiped the ink off the flat surface, then pressed paper against it. The ink that remained in the engraved characters was transferred to the paper, making an exact impression. The copies they made in this way returned with them to France. There, scholars immediately set to work trying to decipher the two inscriptions in Egyptian.

Most started with the demotic section. They assumed that the script would be easier to decode. It wasn't. One expert, Sylvestre de Sacy, managed to identify the group of characters for the name Ptolemy, but he could not tell where one of the linked letters ended and the next began. A Swedish student of his, Johann Akerblad, did even better, spotting several proper names and building up what he thought was a demotic alphabet. After this accomplishment, however, his efforts, like those of other researchers, stalled completely.

In England, a copy of the inscriptions came into the hands of Dr. Thomas Young. Young was a brilliant scientist whose personal wealth allowed him to pursue whatever interested him. He made important contributions in such widely separate areas as color vision, the physics of light, the mechanism of ocean tides, and the nature of astigmatism. Now he turned his attention to the puzzle of the Rosetta Stone. At first, he, too, concentrated on the demotic section. But he could not get much further than Sacy and Akerblad. He decided to try the hieroglyphs instead.

A lot of the hieroglyphic section was missing from the stone, but in what there was, one set of hieroglyphs stood out. They were enclosed in an oval line called a *cartouche,* from the French word for a rifle cartridge, which it resembled. Young knew that the names of royalty were set off from other symbols in this way. Counting up from the end in both the Greek and hieroglyphic sections, he saw that this cartouche must contain the name of Ptolemy.

Ptolemy, *Ptolemaios* in Greek, is not an Egyptian name. As we have already seen, the line of pharaohs with that name were descendants of one of the generals of Alexander the Great, who spoke Greek. What if the Egyptian scribes had had to spell out the foreign name phonetically? Then each of the hieroglyphs inside the cartouche would represent, not a word or concept, but a particular sound or set of sounds. Young lined up the symbols from the cartouche and paired them with letters. To his delight, they fit.

Young now held a clue that might have led him toward deciphering the language. It didn't. The reason was that he still held firm to the belief that hieroglyphs usually stood for words and ideas, not sounds. In his view, a foreign name like Ptolemy was a special exception, because it *had* to be spelled out.

"I HAVE IT! I HAVE IT!"

Jean-François Champollion began life like a hero from a fairy tale. His mother-to-be was 48 years old and very ill. When the local doctors gave up on her, a sorcerer was brought in to treat her. He announced that she would soon give birth to a son, who would be a light of the centuries to come. Jean-François was born soon afterward. He came by an involvement with Egypt naturally. His older brother, a librarian, had applied for Napoleon's team of scholars but had not been accepted. He encouraged the boy's interest in the ancient world.

Jean-François was still a child when his brother took him to meet the great mathematician Fourier, who had taken part in Napoleon's expedition to Egypt. Fourier showed them some of the antiquities he had brought back, including a copy on paper of the Rosetta Stone. When Jean-François heard that no one could read the hieroglyphs, he told his brother and Fourier that someday he would learn how.

Champollion had an amazing gift for languages. By the time he was 13, he already knew Latin, Greek, Hebrew, Arabic, Syriac, and Chaldean. At 17 he went off to Paris to study Persian and, most important, Coptic. He was convinced that Coptic was a direct descendant of ancient Egyptian, even though it was written in a version of the Greek alphabet. He took his studies very seriously. When he was 18, he wrote his brother:

> *I am so much a Copt that I translate every thought that occurs to me into Coptic, just for the practice . . . I want to be as comfortable in Egyptian as in my own French because Egyptian will be the basis for my great work on the papyri.*

Champollion finished his studies in Paris and returned to Grenoble, the town just south of the French Alps where his brother was a librarian. Not yet 20, Champollion was named assistant professor of ancient history at the university and began work on his first book, *Egypt Under the Pharaohs.* His career was off to a brilliant start . . . but it soon came to just as spectacular a halt.

In 1815 the defeated emperor Napoleon returned to

France from his exile on the island of Elba. His supporters, by the millions, rallied to him. One of these was young Jean-François Champollion. The story goes that Champollion tore down the flag of the Bourbon kings from the fortress of Grenoble with his own hands. When Napoleon passed through town on his way to Paris, the young Egyptologist was presented to him. Napoleon learned that he was writing a Coptic dictionary and encouraged him to publish it. After Napoleon's defeat at Waterloo, Champollion's political activities caused him to lose his post at the university. He was fortunate that they did not cause much worse difficulties. Out of a job, he went to live with his brother in Paris and started to work full-time on the problem of reading hieroglyphs.

Champollion knew of Young's work, but he went further than the English scientist. He was sure that hieroglyphs, or at least *some* hieroglyphs, formed a phonetic alphabet. But how could he prove it?

Ptolemy's was the only royal name on the Rosetta Stone. However, in 1822 Champollion found an inscription from an obelisk on the island of Philae that gave the names, in both Greek and hieroglyphs, of pharaoh Ptolemy VII (the younger son of the Rosetta Stone Ptolemy) and his queen, Cleopatra II (not the famous Cleopatra; the Ptolemaic dynasty had a limited imagination when it came to names). Several of the hieroglyphs were the same in both names. Under the hieroglyphs for Cleopatra, Champollion wrote the letters that he already knew from Ptolemy's name, leaving blanks under the symbols that he didn't know:

1	*2*	*3*	*4*	*5*	*6*	*7*	*8*	*9*
—	*L*	*E*	*O*	*P*	—	*T*	—	—

The same hawk hieroglyph appeared in positions 6 and 9, as it ought to if it represented an *a* sound. That left only 1 and 8 to be guessed at. Champollion wrote in a *K* (in Greek, Cleopatra starts with a *K*) and an *r*:

1	*2*	*3*	*4*	*5*	*6*	*7*	*8*	*9*
K	*L*	*E*	*O*	*P*	*A*	*T*	*R*	*A*

Champollion now knew the phonetic meanings of a dozen different hieroglyphs. When he tried applying them to a new cartouche, he got:

1	*2*	*3*	*4*	*5*	*6*	*7*	*8*	*9*
A	*L*	—	*S*	*E*	—	*T*	*R*	—

Symbol 3 was one he had occasionally seen as the first in Cleopatra's name, and Young had suggested earlier that symbol 6 represented the sound *n*. Since many Greek names end in *s*, Champollion guessed that the last symbol represented it. This gave him:

1	*2*	*3*	*4*	*5*	*6*	*7*	*8*	*9*
A	*L*	*K*	*S*	*E*	*N*	*T*	*R*	*S*

or the Egyptian spelling and pronunciation of Alexander the Great.

In the next few weeks, Champollion managed to decipher dozens of cartouches from the Graeco-Roman era. His list of identified hieroglyphs grew longer and longer. But now he took on a new, much more difficult challenge. Could he do the same for inscriptions from before Alexander's conquest of Egypt? As a test, he took a cartouche that had been found on a great many temples and monuments:

1 *2* *3*

𓇳 𓄟 𓋴𓋴

Number 3 was a doubled form of the *s* in "Ptolmis" or Ptolemy. As for the first hieroglyph, Champollion guessed that it stood for the sun, or *re* in Egyptian. That left the unknown sign in position 2. He found the same hieroglyph on the Rosetta Stone, in a group that the parallel Greek text suggested might mean "birthday." Champollion's knowledge of Coptic told him that the word for birth was *mes*. When he filled in these hunches, he found he had:

1 *2* *3*

𓇳 𓄟 𓋴𓋴

RA MES SES

Champollion knew the name of Ramses, of course, from the Bible and the surviving fragments of Manetho's chronicle.

A second cartouche also contained the *m-s* and the *s* glyphs, but in this one the first character was an ibis. Champollion knew that the ibis was the sacred bird of the god Thoth. As he pored over the hieroglyphs, he murmured, "Thoth . . . mes . . . s . . ." Then it hit him—the characters must represent one of the several 18th-dynasty pharaohs named Thutmose.

Champollion had met the challenge he had set himself.

More important, he had learned a vital fact about hieroglyphs. They were not, as earlier scholars had thought, purely symbolic. And they were not, as he himself had believed, purely phonetic. They were a complicated combination of both, along with a few extra twists. As he later put it, "It is a script that is at once pictorial, symbolic, and phonetic within the same text, the same sentence, I would almost say within the same word."

Grabbing his papers, Champollion ran to the library where his brother worked. *"Je tiens l'affaire! Je tiens l'affaire!"* he shouted: "I have it! I have it!" Then he collapsed in a faint. He was unconscious for five days. As soon as he revived, he went to work on a paper explaining his discoveries. On September 27, 1822, he read this report to a fascinated audience at the Royal Academy of Inscriptions in Paris. His listeners understood, as he did, that Champollion had discovered the key to the history, literature, and culture of ancient Egypt.

How Hieroglyphs Work

Imagine that English had started out with a system of picture writing. A small insect that makes honey might be indicated by a drawing: ✤. But in time that symbol also comes to stand for other words that *sound* the same. The opening of Hamlet's famous soliloquy might be written, "2 ✤ or ☋ 2 ✤ . . ." (That other symbol is supposed to look like a knot.) As more time passes, the same symbol may also begin to represent the *consonant b*. If you see "✤*r*" you know you are supposed to read it as "bar," or perhaps "beer," while "✤ ➡" would mean "believe (bee-leave)." The symbol might even show up silently at the end of another word, just to make sure you know the word refers to an insect or to something sweet.

Egyptian hieroglyphs have all these possibilities and more. There are 24 common symbols that can be used to represent all the consonant sounds in the language. Some of these seem like vowels in English, but for technical reasons they are considered consonants. Like Arabic and Hebrew, Egyptian does not write out the vowel sounds. The reader is expected to know which ones to insert in the right places. This is one reason there are different English versions of Egyptian words and names, such as the god *Amon, Amun,* or *Amen.*

These 24 hieroglyphs could have been used as an alphabet, but more often than not, they were not. Egyptians preferred to take shortcuts. Take the word *nefer,* which means beautiful. You could write it using three hieroglyphs representing water *(n),* a horned viper *(f),* and a mouth *(r).* You could, but you wouldn't. Instead, you would use a single hieroglyph that represents, no one knows why, a heart and throat, and that stands for *n-f-r.*

Because the heart-and-throat sign represents three consonants, it is called a *triliteral* (three letters). Triliterals and their close relatives, *biliterals* (signs that stand for two consonants), are extremely common in Egyptian. Sometimes, for emphasis or symmetry, they are even used together with the single-sound symbols. For example, the word for happiness is written with the heart-and-throat followed by the viper and the mouth. It looks as if it ought to mean *n-f-r-f-r,* but it still reads as *nefer.*

Because the vowels are not written out, two words that are pronounced differently and have different meanings might look identical when written. To illustrate this, suppose that written English did not show vowels. What if you saw the word *b-r*? How would you know whether it meant beer, bear, burr, or bore? You would—if the word was followed by a little drawing of a glass, an animal, a plant, or an open mouth.

That is exactly the strategy Egyptian scribes used. After a word, they added another hieroglyph called a *determinative*. It was not pronounced, but it offered a clue to what the word meant. Determinatives had another important use too. In hieroglyphic inscriptions, there are no spaces between words. Determinatives helped the reader figure out where one word ended and the next began.

With all these complexities, it is amazing that Champollion was able to get anywhere at all. In fact, it took him only two years after his success deciphering the cartouche of Cleopatra to publish an initial dictionary and grammar of the language of ancient Egypt. Scholars throughout the world applauded what he had accomplished. The French government, overlooking his political past, named him "Keeper of the Egyptian Collections." Later, in 1829, the government sent him to Egypt as the leader of a new scholarly expedition.

Champollion and his team of scholars and artists spent nearly a year and a half in Egypt, exploring the temples, tombs, and monuments. When he returned to Paris, he set to work decoding and translating the mountains of material he had collected. He was still busy with this huge task when he died of a stroke, at the age of 41. It fell to his older brother to finish the tasks that his death had left undone. These included much bigger and more complete versions of his *Egyptian Dictionary* and *Egyptian Grammar*.

Champollion's work provided the tools to decipher and translate the thousands of wall inscriptions and papyrus scrolls that had survived the centuries. Whether these were priestly decrees engraved on polished stone or hasty notes scribbled on shards of broken pottery, the words and thoughts of ancient Egyptians came back to life. Once, the world of Egypt seemed mysterious, unknowable. The work of generations of archaeologists, collectors, and scholars such as Champollion has made it accessible to all of us.

FIFTY CENTURIES OF GRAVE ROBBERS

The three men walked cautiously along the narrow path that clung to the cliff face. Far below them, the ruins of Hatshepsut's great temple at Deir el Bahri slept in the starlight. The year was 1871. A decade later, one of the men would claim that he and his friends had been out that night searching for a lost goat. That was nonsense. The digging tools and the heavy coil of rope they carried betrayed their real mission. They were tomb robbers, and until tonight, not very successful at it.

The leader of the little group, Ahmed Abd el Rasul, stopped. He had just noticed a darker patch hidden in a crevice behind a great boulder. He looked more closely and saw, almost masked by sand, a small opening in the rocks. He picked up a stone and tossed it in. There was a long pause, then a distant, hollow thud. Ahmed eyed his companions—his brother, Mohammed, and a third man from their village of Qurna. They all knew what that might mean. The opening must lead to a concealed shaft from ancient times. And *that* could lead to unimaginable riches.

The men enlarged the hole, then Ahmed crawled inside and lowered himself down into the shaft. He was gone a long time. Mohammed and the third thief began to worry. Suddenly they heard a terrible scream. Ahmed scrambled up the rope. Shaking, he told them that he had barely escaped from an *afrit,* a malevolent demon. The three men hurried home.

After that night, villagers often noticed a nauseating smell on that section of the path. No one knew where it was coming from, and no one was tempted to find out. That sort of stink was a sure sign that an *afrit* was nearby, and it was well known that *afrits* were not tender with people who disturbed them.

Over the next few years, rumors began to spread. Someone, somewhere, had uncovered a royal tomb filled with treasures. Only a few items reached the bazaars and auction houses, but those few were magnificent—illuminated papyri in splendid condition, little blue statuettes called *ushabtis* that were inscribed with the name of a 21st-dynasty pharaoh named Pinedjem.

In the spring of 1881, Sir Gaston Maspero, director of the Egyptian Antiquities Service, launched an investigation. One of his staff was sent to Luxor, just across the river from Deir el Bahri, disguised as a rich tourist and collector. As soon as word spread of his presence, a Turkish dealer named Mustapha Aga Ayat offered to sell him a royal *ushabti* that had clearly been looted from a tomb.

Ayat could not be arrested. He had somehow managed to get himself appointed as consular agent for Britain, Belgium, and Russia, which gave him diplomatic immunity. Even so, from him the trail led quickly to the Abd el Rasul brothers.

They were carted off to prison in chains and questioned under torture. Even after severe beatings, they stuck to their claim to be totally innocent. Eventually they had to be released.

Once the brothers were back home in Qurna, however, a bitter family quarrel broke out. Ahmed maintained that, since he had been tortured the most, he deserved a bigger share of the loot. The others did not agree. And the neighbors, most of whom also made ends meet by robbing graves, as their ancestors had been doing for many hundreds of years, did not appreciate all the police attention that was focused on their village because of the Abd el Rasuls.

Ahmed's brother, Mohammed, realized that at any moment a neighbor or family member might decide to make him the fall guy. His only hope of safety was to be the first to confess. In early July 1881 he went to the local governor. He admitted that, ten years before, Ahmed had come upon a royal burial site at the bottom of the hidden shaft. The story of the *afrit* had been a ploy to keep the riches within the Abd el Rasul family and away from their supposed partner. The morning after the discovery, the brothers had killed a donkey and dumped its body down the shaft to create the foul smell that kept everyone at a distance. Since then, the brothers had been putting valuables from the cache onto the market a few at a time, to keep prices up and suspicion at a distance.

When word of Mohammed's confession reached the Antiquities Service offices in Cairo, Maspero was out of the country, on a visit to Europe. His second-in-command, Emil Brugsch, sailed immediately for Luxor. There, Mohammed led him up the steep path to the cleft in the rocks. As Brugsch later recalled the moment:

> *I was armed to the teeth, and my faithful rifle, full of shells, hung over my shoulder; but my assistant from Cairo was the*

only person with me whom I could trust. Any one of the natives would have killed me willingly, had we been alone, for every one of them knew better than I did that I was about to deprive them of a great source of revenue.

A great source indeed. At the bottom of the shaft, Brugsch found himself in a gallery choked with:

cases of porcelain funeral offerings, metal and alabaster vessels, draperies, and trinkets. A cluster of mummy-cases came to view in such number as to stagger me. They contained the mummies of royal personages of both sexes; and yet that was not all. Plunging on ahead, I came to the chamber, and there, standing against the walls, or lying on the floor, I found even a greater number of mummy-cases of stupendous size and weight.

By feeble candlelight, Brugsch looked around and realized that the coffins were inscribed with the names and titles of pharaohs of the 18th and 19th dynasties. As Maspero later wrote:

The fellahin *[natives] had unearthed a catacomb crammed with pharaohs. And what pharaohs! The most famous, perhaps, in the entire history of Egypt: Thutmose III and Seti I, Ahmose the Liberator and Ramses the Great. Monsieur Emil Brugsch, coming so suddenly into such an assemblage, thought that he must be the victim of a dream.*

In all, the gallery and chamber contained the mummies of almost forty kings and queens, together with princes, princesses, royal grandchildren, and important court officials. Scattered around were boxes of *ushabtis,* jars in bronze, alabaster, and limestone, papyrus scrolls, and countless smaller items of burial equipment. And who could even guess what treasures the Abd el Rasul brothers had already taken away and sold on the black market to European collectors?

Now Brugsch had, not only a world-class discovery, but a world-class problem. Should he seal the opening and wait for his superior, Maspero, to return to Egypt? Like any serious archaeologist, Maspero would want to see the tomb in exactly the state that Brugsch had found it. On the other hand, Brugsch knew very well what might happen. The local police were not famed for their honesty. Even if Brugsch put his own armed guard at the entrance—and even if the guard resisted the inevitable bribes—the tale of these incredible riches would spread. Every vagabond, crook, and tomb robber for miles would descend on the site. Sooner or later the guard would be outwitted or overcome. By the time Maspero returned from Europe, all Brugsch would have to show him would be an empty cave and an unbelievable tale of the treasures he had missed.

Brugsch was determined to prevent such a fiasco. The next morning he put a crew of over three hundred laborers to work emptying the chamber. It was quite a job. One of the stone mummy cases, that of queen Ahmose Nefertari, was over ten feet long. It took sixteen men just to lift it, and careful maneuvering to inch it through the narrow opening.

Gradually the area at the base of the cliff became jammed with the remains of 3,000-year-old royalty. When the mummy of Ramses I was left too long in the summer sun, the heat made its arm contract, raising the hand slowly into the air. When Brugsch's crew saw that, most of them tried to quit on the spot.

Over the next five days, the cave was emptied and the precious contents carried on board a waiting steamboat. The boat began to move downstream to Cairo. Word had spread of the cargo it carried. For the entire length of the journey, local people lined the banks of the Nile. Women wailed and tore their hair. Men fired their rifles into the air. They were saluting the passage of the dead kings of Egypt, much as their distant ancestors might have done three millennia before. Or were they simply angry and disappointed that such a great treasure was slipping through their fingers?

There was a sequel to this discovery at Deir el Bahri. For leading Brugsch to the find, Mohammed Abd el Rasul received a big reward (which he prudently shared with his brothers) and was hired as a foreman by the Antiquities Service. A few years later, he led archaeologists to another site nearby. There they found the mummies of over 150 high priests of the great temple of Amen-Re at Karnak. This time Mohammed's reward was less generous. The authorities, suspecting that he and his family had found the priests' tomb much earlier and kept it secret in order to loot it, fired him.

The Thieves of Thebes

Imagine that a college outing club, while exploring a cavern in the hills of western Maryland, stumbled across the coffins of Washington, Jefferson, Adams, Jackson, Lincoln, and both Roosevelts. Once people got over the shock and joy of finding them, they would certainly start to wonder. *But what are they all doing there?* Why would anybody gather up the bodies of so many important historical figures and hide them in a remote, secret tomb?

The obvious reason for hiding something is to protect it from danger. And the most obvious danger that faced the mummies hidden in the cache at Deir el Bahri was one that loomed over all the illustrious dead of ancient Egypt: eternal destruction at the hands of tomb robbers.

The practice of breaking into tombs and stealing their treasures probably started at about the same moment as the custom of burying great riches with the dead. In the Old Kingdom, an elaborate mastaba or towering pyramid functioned as a huge billboard with the message *Free Gold—Dig Here!* And dig, they did.

Every single royal tomb that has been found by archaeologists had been opened before by looters, usually only years or even days after it was sealed. Even the tomb of Tutankhamen, so choked with treasures that its modern discoverers needed years to explore and empty it, had had a hurried visit from tomb robbers. They may have been frightened off by guards as they were getting down to work, and for some reason they never returned.

The guerrilla war between the protectors of tombs and the thieves continued throughout the 3,000 years of the Egyptian kingdom and the 2,000 years since that kingdom fell. Whenever the country was stable, with a strong government, a combination of vigilance and heavy punishment kept the grave robbers in check. As soon as central authority began to slip, however, the bands of thieves sprang back to life. Often they had inside information and protection from the same officials who were supposed to be guarding the treasures of the dead pharaohs.

By the time of the New Kingdom, Egyptian royalty had stopped advertising their burial sites. They still built grand funerary temples along the river (or appropriated the temple of some earlier ruler). Their mummies and riches, though, were placed elsewhere, out of sight. Instead of pyramids that dominated the landscape for many miles around, they began to construct elaborate tombs dug deep into solid rock. The entrances were hidden. Within was a maze of corridors, false doors, concealed chambers, and cunning traps. Many of these tombs were in the desolate wadi known as the Valley of the

Kings, on the west bank of the Nile across from royal Thebes.

During most of the 500 years of the New Kingdom, the tombs in the Valley of the Kings were reasonably secure. However, when the power of the pharaohs began to decline, toward the end of the 20th dynasty, tomb robbing again became a major problem. A papyrus that has survived from the reign of Ramses IX (1142–1123 BC) tells of an important court case that involved the mayors of East Thebes, the royal capital, and West Thebes, where the tombs and funerary temples were located. It seems that the mayor of West Thebes was himself deeply implicated in looting royal tombs. He escaped punishment because he enjoyed the protection of the vizier, one of the highest officials in the kingdom.

By the end of the 20th dynasty, the problem was no longer one of protecting the treasures that had been buried with the mummified pharaohs. Most of the treasures had already been stolen. Now the most important question was how to protect the mummies themselves, the sole guarantee of survival in the afterlife. The tomb robbers had already shown that they would set fire to a wooden inner coffin, with the mummy still inside, just to salvage the gold leaf that decorated it. Some had even used the mummies of royal children as torches to light their raids.

Finally, in desperation, a band of devout priests and dedicated officials collected all the royal mummies they knew of in the Valley of the Kings. Secretly, hastily, they moved them to two hidden locations. One was the still secure tomb of Amenhotep II, also in the Valley of the Kings. The other was a few miles away, above Deir el Bahri, in a tomb that had been dug for an 18th-dynasty queen, then abandoned. The mummy cases were crammed into these hideouts, stacked any way. And there the remains of the great New Kingdom pharaohs would stay, undisturbed, for 3,000 years, until the night Ahmed Abd el Rasul tossed a rock through a half-hidden hole in the cliff face.

The Book of Hidden Pearls

During the 700 years that Egypt was a province first in the Roman Empire, then in the successor Byzantine Empire, the religion of Isis, Osiris, and Amen-Re gave way to an Egyptian form of Christianity known as the Coptic faith. The old temples were abandoned or turned into churches and monasteries. The old priesthood vanished, and with it vanished the knowledge the priests had passed along for a hundred generations. There was no one left who could read hieroglyphs, no one who remembered why such overwhelming monuments as the pyramids of Giza had been built. The most common idea was that they were the granaries built by Joseph, in the biblical story.

Much had been forgotten. But two pieces of information survived, passed on from parent to child across the generations. The first was that the ancient rulers of Egypt had been unimaginably rich. The second was that they had hidden their riches either inside their temples, tombs, and palaces, or in more secret places in the nearby desert. If a man desired great wealth—and what man did not?—he need only know where and how to look. By medieval times, treasure hunting had become so widespread that the authorities classified it as a profession and imposed a special tax on it.

The effect this had on ancient monuments was predictably ghastly. In 813 AD, a century and a half after Egypt was conquered by Moslem Arabs, the caliph al Mamun decided to take possession of the riches he thought must be inside the Great Pyramid of Khufu. The original entrance, and all memory of its location, had been lost for centuries. That didn't stop Mamun. He simply chose a likely spot on the north side and told his workmen to start hacking at the great blocks of stone.

Eventually the quarrying disturbed the balance of a huge limestone block. It crashed down into one of the interior corridors. Guided by the noise, the workers dug a tunnel that intersected the passage leading to the Grand Gallery and the King's Chamber. They got there many centuries too late to find any treasure. The King's Chamber contained only a gigantic—and empty—sarcophagus. The story goes that the disappointed caliph then arranged to have gold pieces secretly scattered in the King's Chamber. He did not want the diggers to end up empty-handed after their months of hard labor. The original entrance to the Great Pyramid has long since been rediscovered, but visitors still enter by the gash in its north face known as "Mamun's Hole."

Mamun's approach to finding treasure was to pick an imposing monument and attack it by brute force. This approach remained popular—with the addition of gunpowder and dynamite—even into the 20th century. Another approach that was once even more widespread than Mamun's relied on magic. If you knew exactly where to go, what spells to say, what sort of exotic incense to burn, you wouldn't have to dig or blast. The doors to the treasure chambers would open before you.

What if you did not happen to know the proper spells and incense formulas? How could you find out? Easily, by paying a fancy price for a book that explained them to you. One such book has been sold to eager treasure hunters from before the 15th century right down to the present. Its title is *The Book of Hidden Pearls and Precious Mysteries*. The instructions in it are not so easy to follow, but the results are supposed to be guaranteed.

Here is the way to locate "the Thousand Tombs of Heliopolis": When you are at Heliopolis, set off on a Sunday, taking a southeasterly direction for two good miles, until you come near a site named Iahmoum-the-Black . . . Make fumigations there and go a half-mile toward the northeast with your incense on the flames; you will find an enclosure built of stone and plaster like a circular courtyard, which contains the thousand tombs laid out in ten rows . . . These are the Thousand Tombs, in the seeking of which many persons have perished because they have sought them in an ignorant manner without possessing the requisite knowledge . . . Dig at the east of each tomb and you will uncover some masonry. Break it, perform continuous fumigation, and you will find a sloping way that will lead you to a chamber containing a corpse covered by a cloth of woven gold and wearing golden armor. Near him is everything that he possessed during his lifetime. The incense should be compounded of agalloche, stigmata of saffron, dung, carob kernels, sycamore figs. Take a mithgal *of each of these ingredients, grind them fine, moisten them with human blood, roll them into pellets and burn them as incense whilst walking near Iahmoum; the talismans and the hiding-places will thus be discovered. Take what you need.*

As early as the 15th century, the Arab philosopher Ibn Khaldoun pointed out how silly such guides were. "Suppose that a man did want to bury all his treasures and to keep them safe by means of some magical process," he wrote. "He would take all possible precautions to keep his secret hidden. How could one believe, then, that he would place unmistakable signs to guide those who sought the treasure, and that he would commit those signs to writing?"

Ibn Khaldoun may have made a lot of sense, but the treasure hunters were not listening. Even in 1900, Maspero wrote,

> *Scarcely a month passes without some professional magician coming to recite incantations or burn perfumes in front of some scene carved on a temple wall or of some isolated tomb, and then attacking it with a pick or even with dynamite to extract the treasure that he believes is hidden there.*

Hoping to discourage this sort of vandalism, Maspero arranged to have published a cheap edition of *The Book of Hidden Pearls.* He calculated that if everyone had easy access to the "secret" spells, no one would take them seriously. He may have been right. Still, if the guards disappeared tomorrow from the pyramids and the Valley of the Kings, the treasure hunters would be out in force the day after . . . and the chances are excellent that some of them would be armed with pellets of saffron-agalloche incense and much-thumbed copies of *The Book of Hidden Pearls.*

The Patagonian Samson

In the summer of 1803, a new strongman began appearing at London's Sadler's Wells Theatre. He was a handsome young man who stood over six feet six. The finale of his act—maybe there was an element of destiny in this—was a human pyramid. He strapped a sturdy iron framework across his shoulders, then a dozen other performers climbed aboard. While they clung to the ironwork, he strolled proudly, effortlessly, around the stage. The audiences were thrilled. The performer, an Italian named Giovanni Belzoni, was headlined on the theater posters as "The Patagonian Samson."

Ten years later, Belzoni was still a popular attraction in England, but he was beginning to sense that he might do even better elsewhere. After trying Portugal, he and his wife started for Istanbul, the capital of the Ottoman Empire and a city famous for its popular festivals. Stopping on the island of Malta, however, he met an agent for Mohammed Ali Pasha, the ruler of Egypt. Ali was eagerly recruiting European engineers to help him bring his country into the modern age. When Belzoni said that he had developed a new hydraulic device that would allow a single ox to pump as much water as four oxen hitched to an old-fashioned waterwheel, the agent urged him to go to Cairo and demonstrate his invention.

Once in Egypt, Belzoni spent the next two years trying to build a working model of his water pump. He had to overcome reluctant officials, ignorant workmen, mutinous soldiers, and even a close brush with the plague. Finally the model was finished. The pasha himself came to a demonstration. The pump worked exactly as advertised, but Ali refused to go ahead with the project. It was only four times as efficient as ordinary waterwheels, and he had decided he wanted something six times as efficient.

This decision left Belzoni infuriated and broke. At that point he recalled some conversations with a Swiss scholar named Johann Burckhardt. Burckhardt knew more about the Nile Valley than any other European. Among the wonders he had described to Belzoni were the temple of Abu Simbel, far upstream and almost buried beneath drifted sand, and a huge, striking granite head lying abandoned in a ruined temple across the river from Thebes. The head, known as "the Young Memnon," was so beautiful that Burckhardt had urged the pasha to offer it to England's Prince Regent. Ali did not think much of the idea. What monarch, he demanded, would care about being given a big lump of stone?

Now Belzoni approached the English consul at Cairo, who was known to be assembling a collection of antiquities to send back to London. Would he like to add the Young Memnon to his collection? Soon Belzoni was on his way to Thebes. Once there, he hurried to the temple he called the Memnonium (now known to be the Ramesseum). "As I entered these ruins, my first thought was to examine the colossal bust I had to take away. I found it near the remains of its body and chair, with its face upwards, and apparently smiling on me, at the thought of being taken to England. I must say that my expectations were exceeded by its beauty, but not by its size."

The bust, actually of Ramses II, is almost nine feet tall and weighs seven and a half tons. Somehow Belzoni had to move it across three miles of soft earth to the raised riverbank, and do it in the two or three weeks he had left before the Nile's annual flood made the ground impassable. The only equipment he had brought with him from Cairo was "fourteen poles, eight of which were employed in making a sort of car to lay the bust on, four ropes of palm leaves, and four rollers, without tackle of any sort." It took all his knowledge of mechanics, two dozen workmen recruited from the village of Qurna, and frequent gifts to the local officials, but at last the Young Memnon was aboard a boat bound for Alexandria and then London. Today it dominates the Egyptian collection of the British Museum.

Breathing in Mummy Dust

For Belzoni, moving the giant bust was just the start of a new career. He soon returned to Thebes and began exploring tombs in the Valley of the Kings, looking for papyri and other antiquities. The conditions were appalling:

A vast quantity of dust rises, so fine that it enters into the throat and nostrils, and chokes the nose and mouth . . . In some places there is not more than a vacancy of a foot left, which you must contrive to pass through in a creeping posture like a snail, on pointed and keen stones, that cut like glass. After getting through these passages, some of them two or three hundred yards long, you generally find a more commodious place, perhaps high enough to sit. But what a place of rest! surrounded by bodies, by heaps of mummies in all directions . . . The blackness of the wall, the faint light given by the candles or torches for want of air, the different objects that surrounded me, seeming to converse with each other, and the Arabs with the candles or torches in their hands, naked and covered with dust, themselves resembling living mummies, absolutely formed a scene that cannot be described . . . I could taste that the mummies were rather unpleasant to swallow.

Once, exhausted by a long crawl through a low passage, Belzoni tried to sit down for a rest.

When my weight bore on the body of an Egyptian, it crushed it like a band-box. I naturally had recourse to my hands to sustain my weight, but they found no better support; so that I sunk altogether among the broken mummies, with a crash of bones, rags, and wooden cases, which raised such a dust as kept me motionless for a quarter of an hour.

Another passage between two chambers

was choked with mummies, and I could not pass without putting my face in contact with that of some decayed Egyptian; but as the passage inclined downwards, my own weight helped me on: however, I could not avoid being covered with bones, legs, arms, and heads rolling from above.

It was not long before Belzoni had accumulated an entire boatload of treasures. They ranged from small canopic jars, alabaster vessels, and scarabs, to a massive granite sarcophagus and a fine red granite monument from one of the smaller temples of Karnak. Before he could sail with his collection, though, the French consul, Drovetti, a bitter rival of Belzoni, persuaded the local bey to bar Belzoni from buying antiquities in the area.

The response of "the Patagonian Samson" to this ban was prompt and effective. Remembering what Burckhardt had told him, he sailed upriver to Abu Simbel, hired a crew of local workers, and started digging away at the sand that had buried all but the very top of the great temple of Ramses II for over a thousand years. Within two weeks, Belzoni and his companions were inside the temple, marveling at the brilliantly painted walls and the grand aisle lined with huge statues of Ramses as Osiris. They made a detailed plan and a series of watercolor sketches of the interior before returning to Thebes.

Belzoni didn't rest after this exploit. As soon as he was back in Thebes, he returned to his explorations of the Valley of the Kings. There he discovered the tomb of the pharaoh Seti I, the father of Ramses II. This was the first new royal tomb to be found in the modern age. Of course, all the more portable treasures had been stolen many centuries before, but there was still a magnificent carved alabaster sarcophagus. There were also rooms and corridors lined with brightly colored wall reliefs as vibrant as when they were painted in 1300 BC. Belzoni managed to extract the sarcophagus from the tomb. Eventually it was sold to the English collector Sir John Soane, for his private museum. It can still be seen there. Belzoni also made detailed life-size copies of the tomb paintings. These caused a huge stir when he exhibited them in London and Paris.

In just over a year and a half, Belzoni had single-handedly transformed European knowledge and appreciation of ancient Egypt. However, he had not found a way to make a living at it. Most of the antiquities he had assembled went straight into the private collection of the English consul at Cairo, Henry Salt. Salt liked to think of Belzoni as simply his hired hand. In a bid for independence, Belzoni got official permission to search for the lost entrance to the pyramid of Khafre, the second largest of the pyramids at Giza.

Over the centuries, sand and rubble had piled up many feet deep around the base of the pyramid. Belzoni set a crew of diggers to work at the center of the north face of the huge structure. Forty feet down, they reached a stone pavement that had once encircled the pyramid, but still no door. A mixture of reasoning and intuition led Belzoni to dig farther to the east. There the workers uncovered the entrance to a sand-choked passageway four feet high, formed of massive granite blocks. They began clearing it.

After two days, they found the way barred by what looked like a solid block of granite. Then Belzoni spotted a gap where the block met the floor. He realized that the granite block was actually a sort of sliding stone portcullis, fitted into grooves in the side walls and lowered from an overhead pocket in the stone. Using only wooden levers and rocks, he and his workers gradually raised the block. Belzoni, all six feet six of him, squeezed through the gap into the main corridor of the pyramid and reached the main burial chamber. As usual, others had been there before him. The gigantic stone sarcophagus, sunk into the floor, was half full of rubbish, and there were ancient graffiti on the walls. Still, even if Belzoni had not found a stockpile of treasures, he *had* discovered the way into the pyramid. Moreover, he had done it without the destructive methods that caliph al Mamun had used centuries earlier to penetrate the neighboring pyramid of Khufu.

After this new triumph at Giza, Belzoni returned to the Valley of the Kings. This time, however, both Salt and Drovetti had their agents on hand to claim any site that seemed to interest Belzoni. Balked at every turn, Belzoni turned from archaeology to exploration. He led expeditions into the deserts both east and west of the Nile Valley before returning to Europe. A few years later he died of dysentery while exploring in central Africa.

Like his rivals, Drovetti and Salt, Belzoni was part archaeologist and part tomb robber. All of them were driven by the thirst for riches as well as the thirst for fame. National pride played a large role as well. Every European power wanted its own collection of Egyptian antiquities, as a link to the world's earliest and longest-enduring kingdom. Ironically, Belzoni, the Italian, was most responsible for furnishing the splendid collection in the British Museum. Much of British consul Henry Salt's collection wound up in the Louvre, in Paris. As for the French consul, Drovetti, he finally sold the choicest of his finds to the kingdom of Sardinia, in Italy. They are now in the museum of Turin.

"WONDERFUL THINGS!"

In 1867 people from all over the world flocked to the International Exposition in Paris. One of the most popular exhibits was the Egyptian Pavilion. It was easy to find. Just to the left of the minaret of the Turkish mosque was a huge carved stone pylon from Karnak, flanked by tall poles topped with sun emblems. The exhibits inside gave the entranced visitors a glimpse of life in ancient Egypt. The thrill they felt was heightened because they knew all the items—the statues, the mummy cases, the sphinxes and vases and jewels—were genuine relics of the world's oldest civilization. The new state museum of antiquities at Bulaq, in a suburb of Cairo, had been ransacked for the most splendid treasures in its collection.

The empress Eugénie, wife of Napoleon III, came to see the exhibit. The khedive Ishmail, viceroy and virtual ruler of Egypt, personally guided her around. The empress seemed politely impressed. Then she came to the display case that held the jewelry of queen Ahhotep, mother of Ahmose the Liberator, who founded the great 18th dynasty. For a long time Eugénie gazed at the intricate gold and enamel collars and bracelets, the work of artisans from 3,400 years before. Then she let the khedive understand that she would graciously consent to accept the gift of the jewels.

Ishmail was in a very tight place. He had poured time and money into the exhibit as a way to win greater influence for his small, poor, backward country. Imperial France was a great power, and no one had more influence there than the empress. Besides, the custom of giving priceless *antikas* to powerful friends was an old one in Egypt. Ishmail's predecessors had done it all the time. Did he dare offend Eugénie and cause a scandal that might destroy all the good the Pavilion had accomplished? On the other hand, the jewelry of queen Ahhotep was one of the greatest treasures his country possessed. It was as if he had gone to the Louvre and demanded the *Mona Lisa*.

Thinking fast, the khedive found a diplomatic solution to his problem. "Your Majesty must excuse me," he said. "There is one more powerful than I at Bulaq. You should apply to him."

The "one more powerful" was the museum's director, Auguste Mariette. Mariette was a very eminent Egyptologist, but he owed his position as much to his French nationality and his close ties with Ferdinand de Lesseps, the builder of the Suez Canal, as to his archaeological triumphs. If he offended the French empress, he might jeopardize his own future, the future of his museum, and even the future of French-Egyptian relations.

This was not the first time the jewels of queen Ahhotep had made problems for Mariette. Eight years earlier, in 1859, word had reached Cairo of a great discovery at Thebes: the gold-decorated sarcophagus of the queen, its seals still intact.

The Antiquities Service had been set up only a couple of years before. As its director, Mariette had the right to take the new find for the state museum. But having the right and being able to exercise it were different things. Mariette found out that the local governor at Thebes had already broken open the coffin and taken the jewelry. Now he was sending it as a gift to Saïd Pasha, Ishmail's predecessor as governor of Egypt.

Mariette immediately started upriver in the Antiquities Service steamboat. In his pocket was an official order giving him the power to stop and search any boat suspected of carrying antiquities. He intercepted and boarded the governor's boat between Thebes and Cairo. After half an hour of arguing and waving his order, Mariette had had enough. He knocked down several of the governor's men, almost threw another overboard, and seized the gold at pistol-point. Then he rushed back to Cairo to tell Saïd his version of the encounter. He also presented the pasha with a scarab and a necklace for one of his wives. When Saïd saw the trove of jewelry, he was so delighted that he ordered the construction of a new museum building to house it and the rest of the collection Mariette was assembling.

Mariette's revolver wasn't much use to him in dealing with empress Eugénie's demand. Instead, he met it, and all the threats, promises, and proffered bribes that followed, with a simple, immovable resolution. The jewelry belonged to the Bulaq museum. The museum belonged to the nation of Egypt—past, present, and future—and to all the world. The treasures of the past were a public trust to be preserved for future generations, not the playthings of some transitory ruler.

When the Paris exposition closed, Mariette carried queen Ahhotep's jewels back to Egypt. Three years later, after a war between France and Prussia, Napoleon III lost his throne, and he and Eugénie went into exile. Whatever jewelry she took with her, thanks to Mariette, it did not include the royal jewels of an Egyptian queen.

The Buried Bulls of Apis

There was nothing in Auguste Mariette's background to suggest that he would become a pioneer Egyptologist. He was born in 1821, in Boulogne, France, on the English Channel, and received his first exposure to Egypt when he was 22. A distant relative who had taken part in Champollion's expedition died, and Mariette was asked to go through his papers. He became so fascinated with the history, writing, and language of Egypt that he eventually gave up his teaching position in Boulogne and moved to Paris. There he managed to get a minor job in the Egyptian collection of the Louvre museum that allowed him to continue his studies. In 1850 the Louvre sent him to Egypt to assemble a collection of ancient Coptic manuscripts. In Cairo, however, he met disturbing news. The patriarch of the Coptic church, after some very bad experiences with crooked English collectors, refused to have any more dealings with foreigners.

A minor clause in Mariette's instructions from the Louvre authorized him to carry out excavations. He had no permit from the pasha, no experience, and hardly any money, but he was not going to let an opportunity like this get away from him. He bought some basic equipment and carried it to Saqqâra, the ancient burying ground of Memphis. There he set up camp, just north of the Step Pyramid of Djoser.

Nearby, the head of a sphinx protruded from a drift of sand. Mariette had seen others like it in Alexandria and Cairo, and he knew that they, too, had come from this spot.

Suddenly he remembered a passage from the ancient Greek geographer Strabo:

> *There is also a Serapeum at Memphis, in a place so very sandy that dunes of sand are heaped up by the winds; and by these some of the sphinxes which I saw were buried even to the head and others were half-visible; from which one may guess the danger if a sandstorm should fall upon a man traveling on foot toward the temple.*

Mariette was certain that the buried sphinx was one of those lining the avenue that led to the Serapeum, the long-lost burial temple of the sacred Apis bulls. "In that instant," he later wrote, "I forgot my mission, forgot the patriarch, the monasteries, the Coptic and Syriac manuscripts. And so, November 1, 1850, dawned, and thirty-some workmen assembled by my orders near that sphinx which would so radically alter the conditions of my stay in Egypt."

Over the next three months, Mariette's team of diggers uncovered one sphinx after another. In February they reached the Serapeum and found a magnificent statue of Apis. Just then, Mariette's money ran out. The French consul was impressed with the young archaeologist. He advanced him enough money to go on while Mariette appealed to the Louvre and the French government for more support. However, that meant making his discovery public. He'd overlooked the fact that he had never asked the Egyptian authorities for official permission to dig. When they found out, he was ordered to abandon his excavations and hand over everything he had found.

After weeks of diplomatic haggling, the French consul reached an agreement with the pasha. The Louvre could keep all of Mariette's finds up until that time but would have to turn any future finds over to the Egyptians. News of this bargain reached Mariette just as he finally found an entrance to the underground burial chambers of the Apis temple. Once past the sealed sandstone door, he found himself in a long, gloomy corridor, surrounded by the huge granite or limestone coffins of the bulls. All had been plundered in ancient times, but countless relics still littered the floors. Mariette knew that if he turned them over to the pasha, they would be given out to important foreigners and forever lost to Egyptology.

Determined to prevent the loss, Mariette came up with a plan. He placed his packing crates at the bottom of a shaft. By day, his men loaded them with the objects that legally belonged to the Louvre. By night, Mariette went down into the still secret burial chambers and used a concealed trapdoor to put the finest of the newly found relics in the cases.

Some of these were very fine indeed. At the far end of the Serapeum, Mariette discovered an unopened burial chamber from the time of Ramses II. The footprints of the burial squad were still printed in the dust of the tomb, and the sarcophagus still held the mummified bull and rich offerings of gold and silver. These, too, were spirited out and shipped back to France, where they caused a huge stir.

Mariette's discovery of the Serapeum was one of the two or three most important archaeological exploits in Egypt during the 19th century. It made Europeans much more aware of and interested in ancient Egypt and its monuments. It also made Mariette famous while he was still a fairly young man. He returned to France and a more important post at the Louvre. Six years later, de Lesseps talked a new ruler, Saïd Pasha, into naming Mariette *Ma'amour,* or director, of the newly established Antiquities Service and the museum at Bulaq. Now, at last, he was in a position to do something about his most passionate interest, the preservation of Egypt's ancient monuments.

Mariette began an ambitious program of excavation, employing as many as 2,700 laborers. At one point he had digs going on at 37 different sites all up and down the Nile. His methods were enough to give today's archaeologists a lifetime of cold sweats and shaking fits. What counted above all were spectacular finds, to fill the museum and hold the pasha's fickle interest. If getting to such a find meant using dynamite on the walls of a 4,000-year-old temple, so be it. As for the sort of careful observation and recording that is the backbone of scientific archaeology, Mariette had neither the time nor the trained staff for that. This extended to his personal work as well. He never quite got around to publishing his great work on the Serapeum. Then in 1877 the Bulaq museum was flooded. Among the losses were all his notes on the Serapeum.

During Mariette's time, a tour of the Serapeum was a must for influential visitors to Egypt. Mariette himself acted as guide. In the catacombs, hundreds of local children sat motionless along the vast main corridor, holding lit candles. In dozens of rooms on either side, the enormous stone sarcophagi were lit just as dramatically. Each was twelve feet tall, six feet wide, and sixteen feet long, carved from a single block of granite. The smallest of them weighed at least 65 tons.

A ladder rested against the highly polished side of the last sarcophagus. Mariette invited his distinguished guests to climb up for a closer look. Inside the sarcophagus the guests discovered a table set for ten, with silver candelabra, engraved silver goblets, and bottles of French champagne on ice. It was a visit no one would forget.

The completion of the Suez Canal in 1869 meant that Egypt once more held an important place in the world. Mariette was heavily involved in planning and carrying out the inaugural festivities. This included serving as escort to the empress Eugénie on a cruise up the Nile aboard the imperial yacht *Aigle.* Chances are, neither he nor the empress brought up the affair of queen Ahhotep's jewelry, but there must have been a few awkward silences at the dinner table.

Mariette also took on a very different task in connection with the canal opening. As part of the celebrations, the khedive had commissioned an opera with an ancient Egyptian theme. He asked Mariette to coauthor the libretto. The work had its premiere on December 24, 1871. The composer was Giuseppe Verdi, and the name of the opera was *Aïda.*

Mariette died in 1881, in his house next door to the Bulaq museum. His tomb, in the garden of the museum, is a marble replica of an Old Kingdom sarcophagus. On it is carved the legend *To Mariette Pasha, from a Grateful Egypt.*

Greed and Covetousness

Gaston Maspero, Mariette's successor as head of the Antiquities Service, had much to keep him awake at night. The dozens of royal mummies found in the cache at Deir el Bahri (described in Chapter 10) may have been the discovery of the century, but the Bulaq museum didn't have the facilities to handle such a find properly. Worse, the museum and Antiquities Service were government agencies. When the khedive Ishmail's extravagance plunged the country into bankruptcy, they were among the first to suffer severe budget cuts.

Maspero's biggest worry was what an official edict described as "the greed of the local peasants and the covetousness of Europeans." The heritage of Egypt, which Maspero's agency was founded to protect, was rapidly disappearing. As the nation grew, ancient monuments, even whole cities, vanished. The granite was carted off to be used for new buildings, and the limestone blocks were fed to the kilns, to be turned into lime for mortar. *Sebakhîn* dug up 4,000-year-old mud-brick walls and crumbled them for fertilizer. Whole catacombs of mummies were ransacked for their amulets and scarabs, then discarded or burned.

The plunderers took pride in their ability to outwit Maspero's few underpaid inspectors. One of the most flagrant offenders was an Englishman named E. A. T. Wallis Budge, who had close ties to both the British Museum and the British royal family. His was a simple secret: He paid well for antiquities and asked no awkward questions about where they had come from. His influence even let him enlist the British army in his schemes. The Royal Engineers supplied the equipment he needed to remove large, heavy statues. Budge once sneaked 17 packing cases of antiquities out of the country labeled as military baggage. One carved stone block weighed nearly a ton; he and his officer friends nailed railway ties around it, then disguised the bulky bundle under canvas painted with military markings.

The greatest treasure Budge's tomb robbers found for him was a beautifully illuminated papyrus scroll over 78 feet long, the longest such scroll ever found. It contained a complete text of the Book of the Dead that had been prepared in the 18th dynasty for "the Osiris Ani, the true royal scribe and accountant of the holy offerings of all the gods." After examining the scroll and agreeing on a price, Budge sealed it in a tin box and hid it, along with the many other items he had acquired, in the cellar of his Luxor hotel.

None too soon. That afternoon police under the direction of the Antiquities Service arrested him and cordoned off the neighborhood around the hotel, where most of Luxor's dealers lived. Budge and his friends tried to get the guards drunk. When that didn't work, he kept the guards occupied on the hotel's roof garden. Meanwhile, a team of diggers silently made a tunnel from the hotel grounds into the cellar and carried away the loot. Budge noticed that the diggers seemed to have a lot of experience at this sort of work.

"In this way," Budge later crowed, "we saved the papyrus of Ani, and all the rest of my acquisitions, from the officials of the Service of Antiquities, and all Luxor rejoiced." By all Luxor, he meant the dealers he had been buying contraband from. The following year he sold the scroll to the British Museum, where it became one of the centerpieces of the Egyptian collection.

Budge did not think of himself as a freebooter. Just the contrary. In his view, he was doing the world a great service by saving the heritage of ancient Egypt from corrupt officials and native neglect. As he wrote:

> *The principal robbers of tombs and wreckers of mummies have been the Egyptians themselves . . . Whatever blame may be attached to individual archaeologists for removing mummies from Egypt, every unprejudiced person who knows anything of the subject must admit that when once a mummy has passed into the care of the Trustees and is lodged in the British Museum, it has a far better chance of being preserved there than it could possibly have in any tomb, royal or otherwise, in Egypt.*

Budge went on to remind readers that the ancient Egyptians linked their hope of immortality to the survival of their embalmed bodies. Given all the dangers a mummy faced in Egypt, he was sure that any reasonable Egyptian would have begged to have his mummy carried off to London, where "he is placed beyond the reach of all such evils." Budge was careful not to mention that the scavengers he dealt with were known to destroy an entire tomb and everything in it to retrieve just one mummy they thought would bring a high price.

"THAT GREAT PEACE, THE DESERT"

The young Englishman who arrived in Alexandria in mid-December 1880 had very different attitudes and purposes. His name was Flinders Petrie, and his family tree was thick with scientists and world travelers. Petrie had not had much formal education, but his father had taught him to be a first-rate surveyor. Together they did the first accurate plan of Stonehenge, the megalithic monument on England's Salisbury Plain. In his early twenties, Petrie spent much of his time tramping about the English countryside, surveying important prehistoric structures. A large volume of the plans he drew from these surveys is now in the British Museum.

Petrie's fascination with Egypt dated to his early teens, when he bought a book called *Our Inheritance in the Great Pyramid*. Its author was an eminent astronomer named Piazzi Smyth, who was an old friend of the Petrie family. In his book (which is still in print), Smyth argued that the pyramid of Cheops (Khufu) was so perfect in its dimensions, placement, and orientation that it must have been divinely inspired. He suggested that the strangers who entered Egypt and took it over without a battle (the Hyksos) were ancestors of the Israelites, chosen by God to build the pyramid as a coded message to humanity. Its dimensions, inside and out, represented a divine history of mankind's past, present, *and future.* The key to understanding it was to measure the pyramid using a unit Smyth called a "pyramid inch," equal to 1.001 British inches. British inches, not French centimeters—Smyth was convinced that units of measurement based on the Great Pyramid were God's alternative to the atheistic French metric system.

Petrie's father belonged to a fundamentalist Christian sect that believed in the literal truth of the Bible. In his friend's theories he saw a way of reconciling his beliefs with the findings of science. He was convinced that, according to the Bible, the world was created in 4004 BC. How could humans have built something as imposing and sophisticated as the Great Pyramid only 1,500 years later . . . unless, of course, God directed their hands? The elder Petrie became one of Smyth's most enthusiastic followers. He preached sermons about the Great Pyramid, bent the ears of fellow passengers during train trips, and planned to write a book of his own, elaborating on Smyth's theories.

He and his son also talked about going to Egypt themselves. To understand the divine message of the pyramid, you had to measure it accurately, and Piazzi Smyth was an astronomer, not a scientific surveyor. They did more than talk. Over a two-year period, Flinders Petrie designed and built a complete array of surveying equipment, as precise as any available. For the crosshairs of his theodolites—rotating telescopes used to measure angles—he caught very small spiders and coaxed them into spinning single strands of web. Handmade, custom-fitted wooden cases protected the delicate instruments. In his spare time, what there was of it, Petrie haunted the British Museum, studying the collections of Egyptian antiquities, teaching himself to read hieroglyphs, and picking up some basic Arabic.

Petrie's father never made the journey. Something always came up to stop him. Finally Petrie went on his own. He was 27 years old, with no academic degrees, no sponsors, no official permissions, and very little money. None of that seemed to matter to him. A few days after he arrived, he was camping out in an ancient tomb near the Giza pyramids, surrounded by his boxes of instruments and crates of canned herring and hard ship's biscuits.

Petrie planned to measure and site all nine pyramids—three large and six small—on the Giza plateau, using triangulation. This involved setting up dozens of precisely located stations, then finding the distances and angles between different pairs. In the heat he usually worked in only undershirt and drawers. Not only was this cooler, it also kept curious tourists at a wary distance. While measuring the hot, stuffy interior corridors of the pyramid, he often did without the shirt and drawers as well.

Soon Petrie found himself in a dilemma. His work showed that Piazzi Smyth's measurements of the Great Pyramid were flawed. Those measurements were the basis of Smyth's theory of divine inspiration; if they were off, so was the theory. At first Petrie wrote regularly to Smyth, keeping him informed, but Smyth's replies got colder and colder. Finally Smyth indicated that he would rather believe his own theory than Petrie's research. Later, when Petrie published his findings, he had to conclude:

> *The theories as to the size of the pyramid are thus proved entirely impossible . . . The fantastic theories, however, are still poured out, and the theorists still assert that the facts correspond to their requirements. It is useless to state the real truth of the matter, as it has no effect on those who are subject to this type of hallucination.*

Petrie might be astonished to know that, over a hundred years later, the same theories, based on the same faulty information, are still circulating.

By the time the summer heat got too great for him to go on working in Egypt, Petrie's enthusiasm for Piazzi Smyth's theories had faded, but his enthusiasm for archaeology and his sense of urgency were stronger than ever. "A year's work in Egypt," he wrote, "made me feel it was like a house on fire, so rapid was the destruction going on. My duty was that of a salvage man, to get all I could, quickly gathered in, and then when I was sixty I would sit down and write it up."

In fact, he didn't wait until he was 60 to write it up. He got started on the voyage back to England. *The Pyramids and Temples of Gizeh,* his first book about his work in Egypt, came out just two years later. He would go on to write almost *100* books and monographs. The list of his pamphlets and articles is over 1,000 items long. The pattern he set that first year continued to give shape to his life for the next 40 years. During the winter and spring he was in the field, supervising some new excavation. During the summer and fall he organized his finds, lectured and wrote about them, and looked for sponsors who would give him the money to go back for the next year's dig.

Not that Petrie needed all that much money to go on with his work. Living rough and cheap was a point of pride with him. One of his assistants in later years was a young university graduate named T. E. Lawrence, who would soon become known worldwide as Lawrence of Arabia. In letters home, he described his living conditions:

> *It's really rather amusing that they [the other assistants] are all in terror of instant death because three people died yesterday in the village, and yet cheerfully eat out of week-opened tins after scraping off the green crust inside . . . A Petrie dig is a thing with a flavour of its own: tinned kidneys mingle with mummy-corpses and amulets in the soup: my bed is all gritty with prehistoric alabaster jars of unique types—and my feet at night keep the bread-box from rats. For ten mornings in succession I have seen the sun rise as I breakfasted, and we come home at nightfall after lunching at the bottom of a 50-foot shaft, to draw pottery silhouettes or string bead-necklaces.*

Petrie's training as a surveyor had taught him the importance of precision and concern for details. This carried over into his new career. Egyptologists before him had hunted only big game—the stupendous statue, the royal mummy, the unique tomb painting or scroll. Petrie was as eager for such finds as anyone, but he also paid close attention to things that others had ignored, such as tools, lamp stands, and broken pots. He collected thousands of specimens of pottery, then carefully charted their styles and where they had been found. From this body of information, he created a sequence that allowed later finds to be, if not given an exact date, at least placed in their correct order.

In 1891 Petrie got permission to excavate at Amarna, site of the capital city built by Akhenaten. He knew he could only hope to hit a few high points. To chart the ruins of an entire city would take a lifetime. Among the low mounds on the sandy plain, he soon found one very large ruin he was sure had been the palace of the heretic pharaoh. A huge hall in the middle had footings for over 500 columns. Almost as soon as they started to dig, Petrie and his crew turned up one of the great artistic masterpieces of ancient Egypt. The floor of the hall was plaster, painted with naturalistic scenes in colors that were still bright after 3,200 years. Fish swam in lakes bordered by clumps of reeds and papyrus. Ducks, startled by a romping calf, flew upward from their nest of lotus blossoms. Bound captives knelt in long rows.

Petrie was determined to preserve the painted pavement. He built an elevated walkway, so that visitors could look without damaging the delicate paintings. He also petitioned the Antiquities Service to build a roof over them. Meanwhile, he covered the whole surface with a thin coating of tapioca water, gently spreading it, inch by inch, with his forefinger. The transparent layer protected the pavement without obscuring its beauty. Before the year was out, he also drew outline copies of much of the pavement and a full-scale copy in color of one small section.

The Amarna pavement became one of the great tourist

attractions of Egypt. Unfortunately, the authorities didn't think to build a path from the boat dock to the site. Each new batch of tourists had to find its way across the fields. After some 20 years of this, one of the local villagers got tired of constantly having his crops trampled. One night he sneaked onto the site with a hammer and smashed the pavement to bits.

Early in his career, Petrie had excavated the mud-brick pyramid of the 12th-dynasty pharaoh Senwosret II, in Lahun. The most important find on that dig had been the village where the pyramid's builders lived. There he found hundreds of everyday items, from tools to children's games and dolls, that shed new light on everyday life in ancient Egypt. Twenty-five years later, he returned to Lahun to search the tombs around the pyramid. All of them had been robbed in ancient times, but as a digger was clearing dried mud from the corner of one, he spotted a tiny bead of gold. Soon it was clear that he had found a major treasure.

For the next week, Petrie's assistant worked in the tomb by day and slept there at night. The threads on which the gold and precious stones had been strung were long gone. All the individual beads and fragments were recorded where they lay, with the aim of reassembling them. Then they were detached from the dried mud and sent to Petrie's hut to be washed, photographed, and classified.

The treasure turned out to be the jewelry of the princess Sit-Hathor-Iunet. The archaeologists found everything a princess might need in the afterlife: a silver mirror with a handle of obsidian and gold, gold-topped obsidian jars for cosmetics, necklaces and armlets of gold and precious stones, pectorals of cloisonné and gold. Most important, they found a delicate golden crown with, at the front, the royal cobra in gold and lapis lazuli. Petrie explained what happened then:

> *[The cobra's] head was missing when the crown first appeared; some days afterwards, in washing the earth from the recess, the head was found. Then one eye was missing. I washed and searched patiently, preserving the smallest specks of precious stone. Soon a tiny ball of garnet appeared at the bottom of a basin full of mud; this—no larger than a pin's head—was the missing eye. Yet the gold socket of the eye was missing. I remembered having washed out a bead of gold which differed from thousands of others; looking, I found it again, and there was the setting of the eye complete.*

On this occasion, as on many others, his patience and determination were rewarded.

During his career of more than 40 years as an archaeologist, Flinders Petrie made more major discoveries in Egypt than anyone before or since. More important, he developed a new approach to the field that stressed painstaking attention to detail and context. And most important, he trained an entire generation of younger Egyptologists, infecting them with his enthusiasm for the past and his commitment to pass on the record of that past to the future. Though he was tireless in writing and lecturing about his finds, he felt most at home in the field.

> *In a narrow tomb, with the figure of Nefermaat standing on each side of me—as he has stood through all that we know as human history—I have just room for my bed, and a row of good reading in which I can take my pleasure when I retire to the blankets after dinner. Behind me is that Great Peace, the Desert.*

The Tomb of the Boy King

During Petrie's excavations at Amarna in 1891, his newest and youngest assistant was a 17-year-old English boy named

Howard Carter. Carter was an unusually gifted illustrator and watercolorist. His background was very different from the usual educated middle-class Englishman in Egypt. His grandfather had been a gamekeeper on one of the estates of a wealthy landowner named Thyssen-Amherst (later made Lord Amherst of Hackney). When Carter's father as a child showed talent as an animal painter, Amherst paid for his training. Later he did the same for Carter as well.

Amherst had an important collection of Egyptian antiquities that he wanted to make more important. What better way than to have his own man on the scene, to alert him to new discoveries? So he paid Carter's way to Egypt and arranged to have him join Petrie's Amarna expedition. Petrie was glad to get a free assistant. He even gave Carter a lot of responsibility, putting him in charge of excavating the site of the great temple of the Aten. However, he didn't think much of the boy's future as an archaeologist:

> *Mr. Carter is a good-natured lad whose interest is entirely in painting and natural history: he only takes on this digging as being on the spot and convenient to Mr. Amherst, and it is of no use to me to work him up as an excavator.*

Carter stayed on in Egypt after his year with Petrie. For several years he worked at Hapshepsut's temple in Deir el-Bahri, making full-scale copies of the carvings and wall paintings. Meanwhile, he was learning all he could about Egyptology. He was just 27 when he was appointed to the important post of Inspector in Chief of the Monuments of Upper Egypt and Nubia. Over the next three years, he discovered several royal tombs. He also took charge of fitting the most important tombs in the Valley of the Kings with iron doors and electric lights. By the end of his stint, he knew every inch of the area.

In 1903 Carter was promoted to Inspector of Lower and Middle Egypt. A brilliant career seemed assured. Then one night a group of French tourists had too much wine with dinner and decided to visit the Serapeum by moonlight. When a guard tried to explain that the monument was closed for the day, one of the tourists slugged him. Carter arrived and told the guards to defend themselves. The Frenchmen lost the fight, but they had important connections. Carter was ordered to apologize to them. Sure that he was in the right, he refused. Even when Sir Gaston Maspero, his boss, begged him simply to mumble a few polite formulas, Carter wouldn't budge. He was fired.

For the next four years, Carter lived in Cairo, barely supporting himself by selling his watercolors of Egyptian scenes to tourists. Then, in 1907, Maspero, who hadn't forgotten Carter, introduced him to the rich, eccentric Lord Carnarvon. The result of their meeting would change the course of Egyptology.

George Edward Stanhope Molyneux Herbert, 5th earl of Carnarvon, was almost a caricature of an English aristocrat. His father had been an important and powerful politician, but he was more interested in fox hunting, yachting, and breeding racehorses. Then he discovered the recently invented automobile. In England these noisy, expensive contraptions still had to be preceded by a man on foot carrying a red flag, but Carnarvon kept his in France and drove it all over the Continent. When the English ban was eventually lifted, his was the third automobile registered in the entire country. His passion for fast driving may have helped inspire the character Mr. Toad of Toad Hall, in the children's classic *The Wind in the Willows*.

While motoring through Germany in 1903, Carnarvon came over the top of a rise very fast and found two oxcarts blocking the road. He swerved onto the shoulder. Two tires blew, and the car flipped over. Carnarvon landed in a muddy ditch with the car on top of him. He survived but suffered serious head injuries, broken bones, and bad burns to the legs. His health was never again the same. When winter came, he avoided the stresses of the English climate by going to Egypt. There, like so many before him, he decided to turn excavator and collector of *antikas*.

In 1906 Carnarvon spent several weeks excavating a tomb near Thebes. All he found was a mummified cat, which he donated to the Cairo museum. He also realized that as an archaeologist, he was a helpless amateur. Maspero agreed. He strongly hinted that if Carnarvon expected any further permits to dig, he had better take on a qualified assistant. Then he introduced him to Carter.

They made an odd couple, the prickly plebeian and the easygoing aristocrat, but they somehow managed to get along and work together for 16 years. Carter hoped to return to the Valley of the Kings, but that concession was still held by Theodore Davis, the wealthy American who had sponsored Carter's earlier digs there. Instead, they began exploring another part of Thebes where many nobles were buried. Over the next few years, they excavated many important tombs and published a sumptuously illustrated book about their finds. Carnarvon's private collection of relics grew rapidly.

In 1914 Davis's license to dig in the Valley of the Kings expired. He did not bother to renew it. He was convinced that the area was exhausted, that everything there was to be found had already been found. Carter saw his chance and grabbed it. At his urging, Carnarvon took up the concession. Then World War I erupted. It was three years before Carter and his patron were able to start to work again.

The Valley of the Kings reached its height of importance during the rich, powerful 18th and 19th dynasties. Archaeologists had identified the tombs of almost all the pharaohs of those dynasties. Carter himself had found several of them earlier in his career. The most important exception was an obscure king named Tutankhamen, who ruled briefly in the confused period after Akhenaten and the Amarna heresy. Not only was the location of his tomb unknown, but practically no antiquities with his cartouche on them had reached the market. To Carter, that meant they were probably still underground, waiting to be found.

Generations of searchers had dug over the Valley of the Kings. Their pits and trenches and heaps of sand and broken stone were everywhere. Carter thought he knew where the undiscovered tomb might be, so he set his crews to work clearing the area right down to the bedrock. If there was a tomb entrance there somewhere, he did not intend to miss it through carelessness. In one corner, the diggers uncovered the foundations of workers' huts, probably from the time of Ramses VI. Carter wanted to dig under them, but he would have had to block the entrance to the tomb of Ramses VI. This was a popular tourist attraction. He decided to come back to the spot another time.

For the next five years, Carter and Carnarvon continued to excavate in the Valley of the Kings. They found nothing. Apparently Davis was right: The Valley had been exhausted. Carnarvon was disheartened, ill, and not as rich as he had been before the war. He told Carter that he was withdrawing his support. Desperate, Carter said that he would pay for another season of digging himself. This impressed Carnarvon. He knew very well that Carter couldn't afford such a gesture. He changed his mind and agreed to put up the money for one last year.

On November 1, 1922, Carter's team began trenching near the tomb of Ramses VI. After charting the layout of the ancient huts, they removed them. By the evening of November 3, they were ready to clear the three feet of soil between the huts and bedrock. The next morning Carter arrived at the site. The diggers were standing motionless, silent and intent. Under the very first hut, they had found a step cut into the rock.

Over the next three days, the workers dug downward, clearing step after step. When they reached the 12th step, they could see the top part of a door. On it Carter found a clay seal stamped with the emblem of the royal necropolis. When he made a tiny peephole at the top of the door, he saw a corridor filled to the ceiling with stones and rubble. Whatever was at the other end, the ancients had gone to a lot of trouble to protect it.

Lord Carnarvon was still in England. With amazing self-control, Carter had his men refill the steps with dirt to ground level. Then he sent Carnarvon a cable:

> *At last have made wonderful discovery in Valley; a magnificent tomb with seals intact; re-covered same for your arrival; congratulations.*

News of the discovery spread quickly. By the time Carnarvon arrived, a little over two weeks later, reporters from the world over were on their way to Egypt. This was just the start of a public fever that would last for years.

Carter's men cleared the stairway again. This time the whole length of the outer door was visible. Carter made two discoveries. A clay seal on the lower part of the door carried the cartouche of Tutankhamen. Whether this was a tomb or merely a storeroom of some sort, at least it belonged to the pharaoh they were searching for. The second discovery was worrying. Parts of the door had been opened and resealed twice in ancient times. That meant tomb robbers. Still, the necropolis guards wouldn't have bothered to reseal the door if the thieves had finished their work.

Clearing the rubble from the sloping passage from the outer door to a sealed inner door took almost two full days. Finally, on the afternoon of November 26, 1922, Carter made a small hole in the upper corner of the inner door and held a candle to it, to test for foul gases. The air escaping from inside made the flame flicker. Carter described what followed:

> *As my eyes grew accustomed to the light, details of the room within emerged slowly from the mist, strange animals, statues, and gold—everywhere the glint of gold. For the moment—an eternity it must have seemed to the others standing by—I was struck dumb with amazement, and when Lord Carnarvon, unable to stand the suspense any longer, inquired anxiously, "Can you see anything?" it was all I could do to get out the words, "Yes, wonderful things."*

The beam of a flashlight showed them three huge gilded couches in the form of monstrous animals. Two life-size statues of a king faced each other like guards. The floor was a terrible jumble of inlaid boxes, alabaster vases, carved chairs, weapons, a golden throne, and even a pile of disassembled chariots gleaming with gold and inlay . . . but no sarcophagus. Where was Tutankhamen's mummy? Then Carter noticed another sealed doorway between the two statues. He suddenly realized that this room, so crammed with priceless treasures, was only part of the tomb.

In earlier times, a Belzoni or a Mariette would have had all those treasures out of the tomb in a few days or weeks, and done irreparable harm in the process. Carter was under heavy pressure to do the same. The press, the authorities, even his patron, Lord Carnarvon, were in a passion of curiosity. What was in the sealed inner room? But Carter had learned archaeology at the side of Flinders Petrie. Every single object in the first room, even the tiniest bead, was to be cataloged, photographed, and treated to preserve it before being removed. Only when the anteroom was empty would they explore the rest of the tomb.

Two and a half months later, Carter and his team reached the door to the inner chamber. A group of leading Egyptologists and prominent government officials assembled in the anteroom. One by one, Carter and Carnarvon pried away the stones blocking the doorway. As the opening grew bigger, the spectators gasped. All they could see was a wall of gold.

What they were looking at was the side of a huge carved and gilded wooden shrine. It nearly filled the burial chamber. Inside it was another shrine, then another inside that, then another. The fourth shrine held a massive sarcophagus carved from a single block of yellow quartzite. Inside the sarcophagus was a set of three nesting coffins in the shape of the mummified king. The first two were made of gold-plated wood. The third and last was solid gold, weighing 243 pounds (110 kilograms). Beneath the lid of this last and most splendid coffin, the head and shoulders of the mummy were covered with a beautifully fashioned portrait mask of pure gold, inlaid with gems.

The Mummy's Curse

As spring came, Carter and Carnarvon started making preparations to close down the excavation for the summer. They had accomplished a great deal, but they were just beginning to understand how much more they had to do. The archaeological work was difficult enough, but they also had to deal with the public and the press.

"King Tut's Tomb" was front-page news worldwide.

Every week requests poured in to visit the tomb. Many were from important, influential people. It was hard to say no. But if they gave tours to every tycoon and opera star, or even every noted archaeologist, how would they ever finish cataloging and clearing the tomb? As for the press, flashbulbs went off every time anything was carried out of the tomb. If there was no news of importance on a particular day, one of the dozens of reporters keeping watch would make something up. After all, he had to justify the expense of maintaining him in Egypt.

In the middle of March, Lord Carnarvon suffered a mosquito bite. The bite became infected. He was rushed to the hospital, but in those days before antibiotics, there was not much to be done. Three weeks later, on April 6, 1923, he died.

Now the reporters really had something to write about. The story spread that Carnarvon was the victim of an ancient curse, "Death comes on wings to he who disturbs the sleep of kings." Some reported that at the moment of Carnarvon's death, a power failure shut down the lights of Cairo. Others claimed that at that same moment, his dog, back in England, gave a pitiable howl and died. Arthur Conan Doyle, the creator of Sherlock Holmes and a convinced spiritualist, blamed Carnarvon's death on elemental spirits created by Tutankhamen's priests to guard his mummy. No one seemed to recall that Carnarvon had been a semi-invalid for 20 years, since his automobile crash.

Not long afterwards, the head of the Egyptian department of the Louvre museum died. Then it was the turn of another member of Carter's expedition. By now the press was in full cry. The death of anyone who had anything at all to do with Egypt was blamed on the curse. A tourist was run over by a Cairo taxi, after visiting the Valley of the Kings? Obviously King Tut's Curse. An Egyptian in London was shot by his wife? The curse again. In all, over 20 deaths were attributed to the mysterious curse.

Oddly, one person who was apparently immune to it was Howard Carter. He spent the next ten years painstakingly clearing the tomb of Tutankhamen of the more than 5,000 relics it contained. He died in London in 1939, at the age of 66.

Almost all the treasures Carter and Carnarvon found in the tomb are now in the Cairo museum, where they fill most of the upper floor. Not the mummy of Tutankhamen. After being examined by specialists, it was encased in one of its gilded coffins, then replaced in the stone sarcophagus in the burial chamber of the tomb. It can be seen there today.

Thanks to the determination of Howard Carter and the earl of Carnarvon, Tutankhamen went from one of the most obscure of Egypt's pharaohs to one famous throughout the world. It is hard to imagine why he would want to curse the men who gave him that renown. After all, as the ancient Egyptian proverb says, "To speak the name of the dead is to restore them to life."

The Beginning of the Story

In December 1997 French archaeologists found the tomb of the wet nurse of Tutankhamen, a woman named Maya. Reliefs on the tomb walls show her with her breast exposed and praise her as one "who fed the body of a god." The tomb is in the necropolis of Saqqâra, 300 miles north of Tutankhamen's tomb in the Valley of the Kings. Alain Zivie, the head of the French team, announced that there were still several rooms to explore in the tomb, including two sealed off by masonry. Would one contain Maya's sarcophagus, or even an inscription that finally makes it clear who Tutankhamen's parents were? As Zivie put it, "This is the beginning of the story. There may be discoveries inside the discovery."

The tomb of another, even more eminent official named Maya is also at Saqqâra. This Maya was the overseer of Tutankhamen's treasury. His tomb was found in the 19th century by the Prussian Egyptologist Lepsius, then lost again under the restless sands. In the 1980s a team led by Geoffrey Martin went on a hunt for it. They found it. First, however, they stumbled across a neighboring tomb that was even more splendid. It had been built for one of the powers behind Tutankhamen's throne, the general Horemheb. The tomb was never used; Horemheb later made himself pharaoh and built another, more regal, tomb in the Valley of the Kings.

The Egyptian collections put together by Europeans in the 19th century are filled with statuary and carved reliefs from tombs in Saqqâra whose locations have since been lost. Martin has published a list of some three dozen high officials of the New Kingdom whose tombs are almost certainly somewhere beneath the sands of Saqqâra. And for every one we know about, there are probably a dozen others who have been lost to memory.

There are plenty of ancient tombs waiting to be found elsewhere as well. In the Nile Delta, for example. Near the ancient Delta city of Tanis, French archaeologist Pierre Montet discovered the undisturbed tomb of a 21st-dynasty pharaoh named Psusennes I. The grave goods were almost as rich and plentiful as those found with Tutankhamen, though the levels of artistry and craftsmanship were not as high.

Even the Valley of the Kings, which experts have been calling exhausted for over a century, still holds some surprises. Back in 1825, an Englishman named James Burton entered a low-lying tomb near the tomb of Ramses II. Flash floods in ancient times had filled the tomb with rubble and silt that had dried as hard as cement. Burton dug a tunnel through the first three chambers, found nothing of interest, and left. In 1902 Howard Carter entered the same tomb, now known as KV5. He, too, found nothing of interest. Then the entrance was buried and its location was forgotten.

In the late 1980s the Egyptian authorities proposed widening the road that leads into the Valley of the Kings. An archaeological team led by Kent Weekes was afraid the new pavement might permanently block an important monument. They brought in the latest in ground-imaging radar, seismometers, and magnetometers. Just two days later, with the help of this technology, they found the lost entrance to KV5. It was in a hillside a few feet back from a row of souvenir stands.

Was the tomb worth the trouble of exploring? Burton hadn't thought so, and neither had Carter. But these earlier explorers hadn't cleared the tomb, only burrowed through it. As Weekes and his team dug out the front chambers, they found many objects bearing the names of Ramses II and of his many sons. Even more exciting, they found corridors that stretched back into the hillside. Burial chambers lined the corridors on either side.

With every year's excavation, the number of chambers climbed. By late 1997, the excavators had found 110 chambers, and signs that there were still more to find. They also found a rubble-filled stairway that seems to lead toward Ramses' own tomb. KV5, the tomb of the sons of Ramses II, has turned out to be the most extensive rock-cut tomb ever found in the Valley of the Kings. And it was almost lost forever beneath a parking lot for tour buses.

Why, at the beginning of the 21st century, do so many people continue to be fascinated by a culture that flourished thousands of years ago? One reason may be that the lives, the ideas, and the beliefs of ancient Egyptians were so different from our own. The mummies, the pyramids, the figures of gods with human bodies and heads of animals and birds—all these seem incredibly exotic and mysterious to us.

At the same time, the Egyptians were recognizably people very much like us. They quarreled, they fell in love, they worried about what careers their children should follow, they wondered about their future in this world and the next. And even while going about their everyday lives, they built great monuments that awed other people of their own epoch and continue to awe us, thousands of years later. This gives us hope. If the Egyptians could do it, perhaps we, too, can pass on to future generations accomplishments that will win the battle with Time.

However, we can also see that that heritage is under constant threat. Tomb paintings from forty centuries ago are being destroyed by sewage leaking from snack-bar rest rooms. Ancient temples are disappearing beneath the rising waters of hydroelectric reservoirs. The spreading cities of today overwhelm and bury the sites of the cities of yesterday. This gives a special urgency to the tasks of the archaeologist: to recover the past before it is lost forever, and to pass along a knowledge and understanding of that past to as many as are ready to receive it.

FOR FURTHER READING

There are thousands of books about ancient Egypt. They range from highly specialized scholarly monographs to expensively produced art books with gorgeous illustrations. The books listed here have been chosen because they are all easily available and are written to be accessible to the reader who is not a specialist but who wants to explore the subject in greater detail.

Aldred, Cyril. *Akhenaten, King of Egypt.* New York: Thames and Hudson, 1988.

Budge, E. A. W. *The Egyptian Book of the Dead.* New York: Dover, 1967.

Carter, Howard, and A. C. Mace. *The Discovery of the Tomb of Tutankhamen.* New York: Dover, 1977.

Fagan, Brian M. *Rape of the Nile.* Wakefield, RI: Moyer Bell, 1992.

Gardiner, Sir Alan. *Egypt of the Pharaohs.* New York: Oxford University Press, 1961.

Greener, Leslie. *The Discovery of Egypt.* New York: Viking, 1967.

Hobson, Christine. *The World of the Pharaohs.* New York: Thames and Hudson, 1987.

Lehner, Mark. *The Complete Pyramids.* New York: Thames and Hudson, 1997.

Macaulay, David. *Pyramid.* Boston: Houghton Mifflin, 1975.

Martin, Geoffrey T. *The Hidden Tombs of Memphis.* New York: Thames and Hudson, 1991.

Mertz, Barbara. *Red Land, Black Land: Daily Life in Ancient Egypt.* New York: Peter Bedrick Books, 1990.

Mertz, Barbara. *Temples, Tombs, and Hieroglyphs: A Popular History of Ancient Egypt.* New York: Peter Bedrick Books, 1990.

Reeves, C. N., Richard H. Wilkinson, and Nicholas Reeves. *The Complete Valley of the Kings.* New York: Thames and Hudson, 1997.

Silverman, David P., ed. *Ancient Egypt.* New York: Oxford University Press, 1997.

ANCIENT EGYPT ON THE WORLD WIDE WEB

Here are a few good places to start in exploring the many web sites that deal with ancient Egypt:

Tour Egypt (Egyptian Ministry of Tourism). More than 4,000 pages on-line, including a comprehensive history, biographies of pharaohs, pictures of monuments, detailed maps, a large section on mythology, and a search engine that includes topics in Egyptology:
http://touregypt.net/

Reeder's Egypt Page (Greg Reeder). Links to many other sites as well as interesting articles on somewhat obscure topics:
http://www.egyptology.com/reeder/

Egypt Culturenet. A comprehensive list of Egyptological collections and museums throughout the world, including a guide to the Cairo Museum with pictures of the exhibits:
http://www.idsc.gov.eg/culture

Centre for Computer Aided Egyptological Research. Links galore, with everything from games to hieroglyphic word processors:
http://www.ccer.ggl.ruu.nl/ccer/default.html

Akhet Egyptology (Iain Hawkins). A "clickable mummy," an introduction to mythology, a comprehensive king list, and extensive information on Akhenaten and the Amarna period:
http://wkweb4.cableinet.co.uk/iwhawkins/egypt/index.htm

The Oriental Institute (University of Chicago). Updated information about ongoing digs as well as historical records:
http://www-oi.uchicago.edu/OI/default.html

Institute of Egyptian Art and Archaeology (University of Memphis). A survey of Egyptian artifacts and a tour of Egypt in color photos:
http://www.memphis.edu/egypt/main.html

Virtual Temple (Christina Paul). Graphic pages that highlight architecture, wall inscriptions, art objects, and a gallery of reconstructed portraits of pharaohs:
http://www.netins.net/showcase/ankh/index.html

Giza Pyramids (PBS). A good guide to what is known about the pyramids:
http://www2.pbs.org/wgbh/pages/nova/pyramid/excavation/

Ramesseum Homepage (Gerard Flaments). The history and exploration of this temple, along with plans, photographs, and a virtual reconstruction:
http://ourworld.compuserve.com/homepages/Gerard_Flament

KV5. This tomb of the sons of Ramses II—the largest rock-cut tomb ever found—was uncovered only a couple of years ago. Keep up with the exploration of its 100 or more chambers at:

http://www.kv5.com

Introduction to Hieroglyphs (Serge Rosmorduc). Just what it says it is:

http://khety.iut.univ-paris8.fr/~rosmord/Intro/Intro.html

The Papyrus of Ani (Egyptian Book of the Dead). The text, transliterations, translations, and commentary:

http://www.sass.upenn.edu/African_Studies/Books/Papyrus_Ani.html

More general sites that deal with archaeology and the ancient world include:

Ancient World Web (University of Virginia):

http://atlantic.evsc.virginia.edu/julia/AncientWorld.html

ArchaeologyNet (University of Connecticut):

http://spirit.lib.uconn.edu/archaeology.html

Exploring Ancient World Cultures (University of Evansville):

http://cedar.evansville.edu/~wcweb/wc101/

CREATING YOUR OWN PERSONAL CARTOUCHE

In Egyptian inscriptions and papyri, the personal and sacred names of royalty were set off from the rest of the writing by a stylized oval loop of rope. Because this shape looks something like a rifle shell, the scientists who accompanied Napoleon to Egypt called it a *cartouche,* the French word for cartridge.

As Champollion realized in 1822, and as we learned in Chapter 9, hieroglyphs can work in many different ways. Some stand for the name of an object or concept (for instance, a *bee).* Often, these also stand for the sound of that name (a bee + a leaf = belief). Some hieroglyphs stand for a particular combination of two or three sounds or phonetic units. However, the ones we'll be using here, shown in the following table, stand for individual phonetic units. They are more or less equivalent to our alphabet.

HIEROGLYPH	REPRESENTS	SOUNDS LIKE
𓄿	a vulture	*a* in *father*
𓇋	a reed leaf	*i* in *in*
𓇌	two reed leaves	*ee* in *reed*
𓂝	an arm & hand	broad *a* in *fat*
𓅱	a quail chick	*oo* in *too* or *w* in *we*
𓃀	a foot	*b* in *be*
𓊪	a mat	*p* in *pass*
𓆑	a horned viper	*f* in *fat*
𓅓	an owl	*m* in *me*
𓈖	water	*n* in *no*
𓂋	a mouth	*r* in *ring*
𓉔	a courtyard	*h* in *hat*
𓎛	twisted yarn	*h!* in *ha!*
𓐍	?	*kh* in Scottish *loch*
𓄡	an animal's belly	*ch* in German *ich*
𓋴	folded cloth	*s* in *see*
𓈙	a pool	*sh* in *show*
𓈎	a hillside	*k* in *keep*
𓎡	a basket	soft *k* in *basket*
𓎼	a stand for a cookpot	g in *go*
𓏏	a loaf	*t* in *top*
𓍿	a rope tether	*tch* in *church*
𓂧	a hand	d in *dog*
𓆓	a snake	*dj* in *adjust*

THE HIEROGLYPHIC ALPHABET

To design your own cartouche, first hunt through the table for the hieroglyphs that correspond to the sounds in your name. Here, for example, is the name *Amanda:*

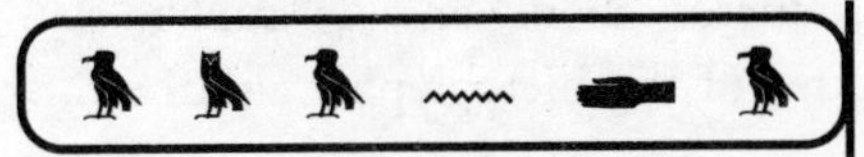

Hieroglyphs can be written from left to right or right to left, just as you choose. Most of the time Egyptians wrote from right to left, but we are so much in the habit of reading from left to right that we usually find it easier to write that way too. If you prefer, you can also write hieroglyphs from the top down. Much more rarely, they are even written from the bottom up. If you are wondering how to tell which way to read an inscription, there are two important clues. First, any living beings, such as birds and animals, face the *beginning* of a name. Second, the knotted end of the rope looped around a cartouche is at the *end* of the name. In the two cartouches below, the first one reads from left to right, while the second one reads from right to left.

If designing your own personal cartouche has left you wanting to find out more about hieroglyphs, here are two recent introductions:

Wilson, Hilary. *Understanding Hieroglyphs: A Complete Introductory Guide.* New York: Passport Books, 1995.

Zauzich, Karl-Theodor. *Hieroglyphs Without Mystery: An*

Introduction to Ancient Egyptian Writing. Austin: University of Texas Press, 1992.

For kids (and adults with a playful streak), a museum curator of Egyptian art has put together a kit that includes an introductory book and 24 rubber stamps, one for each letter of the hieroglyphic alphabet:

Roehrig, Catherine. *Fun With Hieroglyphs.* New York: Penguin, 1990.

Those who find books less involving than searching out information on the Internet can point their browsers to a site maintained by a French Egyptologist, Serge Rosmorduc, at: http://khety.iut.univ-paris8.fr/~rosmord/Intro/Intro.html

INDEX

INDEX

ABOUT THE AUTHOR

IAN McMAHAN has been fascinated by the ancient world since childhood, when a school librarian handed him a copy of the classic *Gods, Graves, and Scholars.* A faculty member at Brooklyn College, City University of New York, his other works include a novel, *Footwork,* and the Microkid mystery series for children. His book *Get It Done! A Guide to Motivation, Determination, and Achievement* was recently published by Avon Books. This is his first book on Egypt.

WITHDRAWN
PRINTED IN U.S.A.
GAYLORD